A DECENT LIFE

A DECENT LIFE

Morality for the Rest of Us

TODD MAY

THE UNIVERSITY OF CHICAGO PRESS *Chicago and London*

The University of Chicago Press, Chicago 60637
The University of Chicago Press, Ltd., London
© 2019 by The University of Chicago
All rights reserved. No part of this book may be used or reproduced in any
manner whatsoever without written permission, except in the case of brief
quotations in critical articles and reviews. For more information, contact the
University of Chicago Press, 1427 E. 60th St., Chicago, IL 60637.
Published 2019
Printed in the United States of America

28 27 26 25 24 23 22 21 20 19   1 2 3 4 5

ISBN-13: 978-0-226-60974-4 (cloth)
ISBN-13: 978-0-226-60988-1 (e-book)
DOI: https://doi.org/10.7208/chicago/9780226609881.001.0001

Library of Congress Cataloging-in-Publication Data

Names: May, Todd, 1955– author.
Title: A decent life : morality for the rest of us / Todd May.
Description: Chicago ; London : The University of Chicago Press, 2019. |
Includes bibliographical references and index.
Identifiers: LCCN 2018031101 | ISBN 9780226609744 (cloth : alk. paper) |
ISBN 9780226609881 (e-book)
Subjects: LCSH: Ethics. | Conduct of life.
Classification: LCC BJ1012 .M385 2019 | DDC 170/.44—dc23
LC record available at https://lccn.loc.gov/2018031101

♾ This paper meets the requirements of ANSI/NISO Z39.48-1992
(Permanence of Paper).

CONTENTS

PREFACE

You're a good person. The fact that you even picked up this book is proof. Acting decently toward others matters to you. And yet consider Matt Wage, a promising undergraduate student at Princeton who wanted to continue his studies in philosophy. Matt decided that a career in a field he loves would not contribute enough good to the world, so instead he became a Wall Street arbitrage trader. As a trader, he reasoned, he could donate half or more of his earnings to charity. Or pause a moment over Alexander Berger, a student at Stanford University, whose research showed that donating a kidney, despite being a very unpleasant procedure, is not a threat to one's health. A long list of people are awaiting kidney donations, so he decided to donate one of his.[1]

This is a book of philosophy, not for Matt Wage or Alexander Berger but for the rest of us. It is a book of morality. It is an attempt to frame a way of moral living that I have called "decency." Most of us seek to live a morally decent life. We are not moral monsters, but neither do we strive to be moral saints. I reflect here on the many decent things most of us already do, but I also point toward avenues of moral improvement that do not require surrendering ourselves to traditional moral philosophy's imperative to live "the best life" or a morally ideal life.

Should you give money to panhandlers? Should you stop eating meat? Should you hold the door for people who never even acknowledge your existence? Should you try to talk politics with those on the other side? Let's think here together about a life with a goal more modest than altruism, but better than moral mediocrity. How can we live a decent life?

ALTRUISM OR DECENCY?

It was rush hour. Waves of people, most dressed in black, moved across one another, toward or away from the metro station. Some were transferring to connecting regional trains or to those slated for longer routes. Others were coming in from the cold outside, heading down long sets of stairs and through cavernous halls toward the platforms. Those people seemed to carry the chill in with them, their breath still steaming as they entered the station. In many ways it was like rush hour in any big city. But when a train arrived at the platform where I was waiting, I noticed something different.

Crowded as the platform was, leaving little room to move, none of the passengers boarded the train until everyone who was exiting had gotten off. There was even a moment of hesitation, a second's pause, before the first passengers embarked. One person near the doors of the train craned his head to look inside, checking to see whether anyone else had yet to alight. Only then was there a general movement to board.

The scene was something I gradually learned to expect in Copenhagen. My experience growing up in New York City was very different. There was impatience to get on the subway, an impatience that I shared. For some, more than a few, that impatience led to a sidelong movement, slicing through the exiting crowd and boarding the train while others were still trying to leave. The idea that there would be a moment's hesitation between the last person leaving and the first one entering was unthinkable. If someone did that we would all be wondering what was wrong with them. Perhaps they were tourists, or just clueless.

In Copenhagen it is not like this. People wait for one another, and not only at train stations. I have never seen someone push ahead of another in line or act impatiently at another's momentary faltering. There, the closest I have come to being berated is in the looks I received when stepping inadvertently into a bike lane. But after all, it can't be fun for a biker to swerve around someone who doesn't know that he is in the middle of traffic.

It's important not to romanticize this phenomenon, both because it isn't that romantic and because it would betray my point. In most respects, Copenhagen is like a lot of other big cities. People do not smile at strangers on the street. There is no sense of overt camaraderie on trains, buses, or elsewhere. While the word *tak*—thanks—is ubiquitous in its various forms for the smallest of favors, or even for expected service (Danes seem to seek out opportunities to thank others), the social feel of Copenhagen will be familiar to those who have wandered through other large urban areas. It is not that Copenhageners, or Danes in general, display a greater warmth toward others than one finds elsewhere. (In fact, I found more public warmth in Athens, and Greeks are not renowned for waiting patiently in lines.) Rather it is that they seem to recognize, or better to acknowledge, that those others are there. Others, just like oneself, have schedules they're trying to meet, plans they're seeking to accomplish, projects that are carrying them forward. I too have a life I am trying to carry on, a life whose requirements have brought me here, to this metro platform, at this moment. But so do these people leaving the train. And that is a fact I should take into account or, even better, inculcate as a natural part of my own behavior.[1] This acknowledgment is the basis—the moral core—of what I am going to call *decency*.

This is a book about that decency. It is not a book about being an exemplary moral person, what is sometimes called an altruist. Nor is it a book about how to fulfill our basic moral requirements, the least we might owe to one another. Much of contemporary discussion of morality seems concerned with such issues, in ways I will canvass in a moment. My concern is different. Simply put, most of us want to be better than moral mediocrities and yet don't see ourselves as altruists; how then might we think about living morally? How might we frame our approach to morality? I use the word *decency* to capture one way to do so. Decency, as I articulate it, is not concerned with traditional concepts in moral philosophy such as duty, right, utility, intent, obligation, or the Good. Or, more precisely, it cuts across all these concepts. I am not interested here in questions of what the ultimate good is or how to conceive our duties or whether we are obliged to craft the best moral character we can manage. Philosophers far more capable than I am have debated these questions across the centuries. My interest is more pedestrian. Most of us are incapable of living lives that are beacons of moral light. Yet most of us also desire to be morally decent people, and we have some more or less inchoate sense of how that might go. Is there some way to frame moral decency that would enlighten us as to what we are up to in some of our better moments, a frame that at the same time might act as a reflective standard for maintaining or even multiplying those moments? Such is the project of this book.

PHILOSOPHY REFLECTS ON MORALITY

Before I unfold my own view, let's pause to consider the current state of philosophical reflection on morality. Even those who are not vocationally immersed in such reflection—which is almost everyone—will likely have at least a breezy familiarity with the moral concepts that characterize current moral debates. For instance, questions of whether the ends justify the means or the importance of intending to do the right thing are familiar to all of us. Philosophical reflection approaches such questions in a more formal way, with different language, but the roots of that reflection can always be traced back to perennial human concerns.

We might divide philosophical moral positions into three types: consequentialism, deontology, and virtue ethics.[2] If we investigate these positions, we will see that they do not give us the guidance we need if what we're after is not altruism but simple moral decency. The first position conveniently announces in its name where it thinks the proper moral stakes lie: in the consequences. This is the position that the ends in fact do justify the means. Of course, not all ends justify any means—which is what some people often mistake for the definition of consequentialism. Rather, it is the view that we ought to act in a way that promotes the most good (however "good" is defined) at the lowest moral cost. If this sounds like an economic version of morality, it should. Consequentialists would like to incorporate all the (alleged) precision of economics into moral decision-making. Plus, they believe that ultimately results are what matter. To put it another way, the moral bottom line for consequentialists lies in contributing to making the world a better place.

Consider this example. You want to break up with your boyfriend. You care for him, but you know that this is not going to work out in the long run. He's a really nice guy, and attractive, but in the end just a bit too boring. Or he holds political or religious views that get on your nerves. Or he allows his mother to intrude on your relationship in ways that you just cannot abide. But here's the problem. He's really into you, and you know that breaking up with him will make him suffer. Moreover, in breaking up it will be *you* who makes him suffer. You will be responsible. You would really rather that things end differently. Maybe you could make yourself unpleasant around him so he would break up with you instead. Or perhaps there is somebody you could introduce him to that would capture his fancy. Or, as a last resort, maybe time will take care of it without your having to do anything.

In the end, though, you know that relying on any of these alternatives is not likely to work out and that the longer you allow this relationship to drag on, the worse it will be in the long run for both of you. Better to break up now, cause the suffering he will inevitably endure, and then allow him as well as you to move on. The result—less suffering overall— justifies the means—suffering in the short term.

This is an easy case. There are much more difficult ones that we all could think of, such as whether to agree with a friend about an important, but false, belief they have if you fear it will cause them her pain to learn the truth or, on a larger scale, whether to place some civilians at greater risk during war time to save a larger number of civilians. However, although the calculations may become complex, the approach does not differ. Consequentialist moral assessment focuses on the most good that can be achieved at the least cost. The point of morality for consequentialists is to improve the world's conditions, and such calculation determines the best way to do it.

I should note in passing that consequentialism—like other moral approaches—does have some odd, well, consequences. In fact, all moral theories have their quirks. If some moral view came along that didn't, it would probably knock all the other competing theories out of contention. One of the quirks of consequentialism is that it allows for what is sometimes called moral luck. I can do the right thing through sheerest contingency, perhaps even when I'm trying to do the wrong thing. Suppose, for instance, that I offer to teach someone in my office the new computer program that has just been installed. In fact, I have no intention of teaching it to him, but instead plan to keep putting off the teaching so that my colleague will fall behind and get a worse evaluation than I will. However, my supervisor overhears my offer and then realizes that she should set up a training session for the new program for everyone. My action, although aimed toward a bad consequence, has actually had a good one. And so, by the lights of consequentialist theory, it is a good act.

Deontological theory, which focuses on people's intentions or actions rather than consequences, would instead consider such underhanded behavior morally bad. For the deontologist, the means rather than the end is the morally salient characteristic of an action. What makes an act right or wrong is the intention behind it or the way it came about. To see this, we can look at the view of the classic deontologist, Immanuel Kant. For Kant, an act is the right one only if it conforms to what he calls the "categorical imperative." The imperative has several formulations, but the most often invoked one is "Act only on that maxim through which at the same time you can will that it should become a universal law."[3]

What does this mean? We can understand it more clearly if we look back at our two examples. Should you break up with your boyfriend, whom you do not love? In this case Kant would offer the same answer as the consequentialist—you should—but for a very different reason. It's not that it would cause more suffering to delay the breakup, but rather in delaying it you are acting dishonestly with him. And you cannot will dishonesty to a universal law, at least not without contradicting yourself.[4] Think of it this way. If everyone were dishonest, then no one would trust anyone else. And if no one trusted anyone else, dishonesty would lose its point. Dishonesty works only against a background of trust. If you don't trust me I can't mislead you with my dishonesty. So if everyone were dishonest—that is, if dishonesty were a universal law—then dishonesty would lose its very point. So, Kant says, you cannot rationally will dishonesty to be a universal law. And if you can't do that, it is morally forbidden to act dishonestly.[5]

Deontology, in contrast to consequentialism, is not concerned with the results of the way one acts but rather with the intentions or means that animate it. This would lead Kant to the opposite assessment of my misleading my colleague about teaching him the computer program. Yes, Kant would argue, the act inadvertently had good consequences, but the intention behind the act—once again, dishonesty—could not consistently be willed as a universal law. Therefore the act was morally wrong.

Kant's view, like consequentialism, has its quirks. Consider this one. When I started going bald, I found it disturbing.

(Eventually I began to shave my head in a sort of "You can't fire me because I quit" response.) My wife was merciful enough to deny the obvious. No, she assured me, it didn't seem to her that I was losing my hair. *I* knew what was happening, since there are mirrors in my house. But she was letting me down easy, and in doing that by lying was violating Kant's categorical imperative. In other words, she was acting immorally.

There are more serious quirks as well. A classic case in the philosophical literature is this one. You've made an appointment to meet a student, promising them you will be in your office at a certain time to discuss their grade on a recent paper. On the way there you see somebody get hit by a car. They're lying in the street and you can aid them, but it will make you miss your meeting. If you follow Kant's moral view, you must meet the student instead of helping the victim of the accident, since you cannot will breaking a promise to be a universal law.

The quirks I have cited for both consequentialism and deontology are not meant to be decisive refutations of their views. There are reams written about how to deal with these quirks, or whether—as in the case of moral luck—they are a problem at all. Rather, my point here is to note that there is not a straightforward path from these views in their simple form to moral practice, a point that will have bearing for us in a bit. So it should be no surprise that the third leading theory, virtue ethics, has its own complications.

Originally drawn from the ancient philosopher Aristotle, virtue ethics has been enjoying a renaissance in philosophy over the past thirty years or so. What distinguishes virtue ethics from consequentialism and deontology is its shift of moral concern from focusing on acts to focusing on the moral status of oneself. We might say that if the key question for consequentialism and deontology is "How should I act?" then the key question for virtue ethics is "How should I live?"[6]

Aristotle argues that the good life is one of *eudaemonia*, often translated as "happiness" but perhaps better rendered as "flourishing." What is this good life of *eudaemonia*? For Aristotle, "the human good proves to be activity of the soul in accord with virtue."[7] To live well is to cultivate and express different virtues, such as bravery, temperance, wisdom, and generosity. Famously, these are means between extremes. For instance, bravery is a mean between rashness and cowardice. This does not imply that it is somehow halfway between the two. Rather, it is properly situated between them in a way that the virtuous person will understand. Moreover, Aristotle thinks that virtues are complementary to one another. Cultivating each of them will help us to cultivate the others; there is no conflict among them.

As is often noted, the assumption that virtues will not conflict is a shaky one. Bravery, for instance, does not necessarily help us become more temperate. In fact, there could be tensions between the two, as when performing a brave act requires me to lay aside my temperance and focus on the dangers I'm confronting. But even if we abandon this assumption, we should still ask how much guidance a theory like this can give us in our moral lives. Yes, we might become better people through being more temperate or wise or generous, but how do we do that and where in our lives are we supposed to display this or that virtue? There seems to be some distance between the virtues that Aristotle recommends to us and the answer to the question of how one should live.

This is not to say that the distance cannot be bridged. But even if it can, it leaves a deeper question, one that is characteristic of all three moral approaches. Aristotelean virtue ethics offers an account of how we should live. Consequentialism and deontology offer us views of how we should act. Each of these views is an account of what a proper moral existence would consist in. Each tells us what we should do or how we should live. We might ask which of these views is more nearly right. Philosophers do that all the time. My concern here is different. No matter which view we pick, we will find it difficult to live up to its requirements. Very difficult. In dictating the proper moral form of our existence, all these theories ask more than most of us are capable of. This is not hard to see.

To be a consequentialist, for instance, is to be concerned always with the best consequences of one's actions. That involves a lot of sacrifice. Am I really to count my own interests, as well as those people I care about, as having no more of a grip on me than the interests of others? Am I to be expected always to abandon my commitments to those I love or to those projects I'm committed to when it would do more good to do so? That is certainly asking a lot of me.[8]

But it seems to be no less demanding than holding the categorical imperative to be the only source of my moral existence. Perhaps I shouldn't help a friend of mine cheat on his exams or claim more hours at work than he has actually put in, but must I really keep a promise to go to the movies with my brother when, on the way to the theater, I get a call from an acquaintance in deep distress who just needs someone to talk to? Or can I never act in a way that benefits me at the expense of another? Am I to treat everyone around me with the same moral solicitude that I treat my friends?

Or in virtue ethics does the cultivation of virtues have no letup? Does it allow for no moral holidays? Aristotle himself recognized the difficulty of living the good life, even though he thought it was the *telos*—the goal—of being human. It requires rigorous training in an environment conducive to

developing the habits each of the virtues requires. It also requires friends, adequate material resources, and a physical
appearance that is at least not ugly. Moreover, he seems to
doubt that most of us will get there. While not impossible,
it seems that the good life, the life of *eudaemonia*, is difficult
to attain and often difficult to maintain over the course of
a lifetime.

From the perspective of all these theories, the moral life is
a difficult one. It requires a great deal of sacrifice and focus,
often turning us away from our most important commitments and toward ways of living that, while admirable, are
onerous or even impossible for many of us to achieve.

DOES TRADITIONAL MORAL PHILOSOPHY ASK TOO MUCH?

Are the moral burdens these views place upon us unnecessary or unfair? Maybe instead we should just live different
lives from the ones most of us inhabit now. Does the difficulty of embracing one or another of these moral theories tell
against them? Perhaps the problem lies not in the theories.
Perhaps it lies in us, in our own unwillingness to commit
ourselves to better lives. Perhaps, rather than rejecting the
prescriptions of these moral theories as beyond our capacities, we should learn to develop those capacities to meet the
challenges the theories present to us. If morality indeed does
ennoble us, our proper task might well be to make ourselves
more noble that we currently strive to be.

One of the most famous of contemporary moral philosophers, Peter Singer, has offered an argument for an extreme
form of altruism that still has a grip on many people today.
In his seminal article, "Famine, Affluence, and Morality," he
provides us with an indelible image: "If I am walking by a

shallow pond and see a child drowning in it, I ought to wade in a pull the child out. This will mean I will get my clothes muddy, but this is insignificant, while the death of the child would presumably be a very bad thing."[9]

We can all agree that I should pull the child out of the pond. It would be irresponsible of me not to. I am deeply obliged to save the child. It is not an act of charity on my part but rather a moral duty. But what is the relevant difference, Singer asks, between the effort required to save this child and the effort required to save a starving child somewhere else on the planet by writing a check to an organization that delivers food to starving children? He argues that simple physical distance can't make the former an obligation and the latter a matter of voluntary charity. Why should geographical proximity be relevant? What moral bearing could it possibly have? I am just as obliged, he argues, to write the check as to wade into the pond. In fact, I might be *more* obliged to the starving child. It costs me less effort to write a check than it does to clean off muddy clothes. If we count the difficulty of the effort to help someone as morally relevant (so, for example, I might not be required to save the drowning child at the risk of my own life), then I should write the check even before I consider wading into the pond.

So far, so good. What Singer seems to have shown us is that we have more moral obligations than we thought we did. But he goes further. After all, there are a lot of starving children I can save by writing checks, and a lot of other children whose suffering I can relieve in many other ways. If it costs me little effort in each case to do so, then why would I be less obliged to each of these children than to the first one? Consider this admittedly strange example. Suppose I muddy my clothes and save the drowning child. Then I continue on my way. But a few minutes later I see another drowning child in another shallow pond. Am I less obliged to save this child than the first one? Is this next child's life worth less, or will my effort to save them be decidedly more? My clothes are already muddy, so in that sense it would be less effort to save this next child. And what of the child after that? (Perhaps it has been extremely rainy recently.) And the following one? And further, what is the difference between each of these drowning children and all the starving children that I can save through writing checks?

You can see where this leads. It is not that there is no end to my obligations. But they don't end very soon. Singer argues, "If it is in our power to prevent something bad from happening, without thereby sacrificing anything of comparable importance, we ought, morally, to do it."[10] This principle tells me where my obligations end: when fulfilling the obligation would require me to sacrifice something "of comparable importance," in this case my life. That's a pretty strict moral principle. Singer thinks it is the right one. But he does concede that a weaker principle might also be applied, that we be willing to sacrifice something up to the point where what we would be sacrificing is "morally significant."[11] The difference here is that on the stronger principle I would be obliged to reduce my level of well-being to something near that of a starving child before my obligation to save starving children would end. Since my life is worth no more than any of theirs, why should my well-being matter more?

However, even if we take the weaker principle, we would still have to sacrifice a good bit. Most of us don't consider eating at restaurants, or buying the occasional nice outfit, or attending sports events, or traveling on vacation, or enjoying an evening drink, or taking our children to a play to be subject to moral criticism. But in Singer's view they are. We can get by well enough without doing any of these things. Even on the weaker principle, then, we would still be required to forgo a good bit. And think of this: in each case we have a particular enjoyment on one side of the scale and the life of a starving child on the other. How morally significant would any of these activities really seem to be then?

If Singer is right, we are obliged to act according to a very strict morality. This obligation is different from the one we saw in Aristotle and Kant. For them, the reason for rigor lay in our essence as human beings. We are essentially rational creatures and so to act on something less than our rationality is a betrayal of our human character. Peter Singer doesn't care about our human essence. What matters to him is simply the fact that each of us is only one among many whose interests have equal moral worth. Therefore we have no moral justification in treating our interests better (or, on the weaker principle, much better) than anyone else's.[12]

But is he right? Are we really obliged to act in accordance with a morality that would ask of us to sacrifice our deepest personal commitments and projects if these conflict with moral requirements, be they consequentialist, deontological, or virtue ethical?

There are reasons to think not. First, consider this.[13] There are aspects of our lives that make them worth living, that contribute to their being meaningful lives. Some of these aspects are individual. There are people for whom painting is so important that their lives would be significantly diminished if they couldn't paint. For others, a life without the opportunity to read novels or watch movies would be a diminished one. I have a friend—fortunately one whose body seems immune to injury—who is convinced he would be existentially at sea if he could not run every day; running is central to his sense of who he is (and it shows in his performance—he is one of the best runners in his age group in the country).

These are aspects of people's lives that are not generally shared. There are other aspects to people's lives, ones that furnish them with the significance they have, that most of us do share. Perhaps chief among these are ongoing friendships and love relationships of various kinds (with a partner, with children, and also with certain close friends). Many of us have careers whose activities help give our lives the point they have. Of course there are elements of any career that don't do that—the tedious parts that one just has to soldier through—just as there are moments in friendships and love relationships that one could do without. But the overall arc of a good career is one that, for someone engaged in it, lends their life a good bit of the meaningfulness it possesses.

If we are asked to contribute to the lives of others less fortunate than ourselves, presumably this is because it will make their lives more worth their living. We should contribute to feeding someone who is starving, for instance, not simply to feed them but to allow them to live in a way that is meaningful to them. To feed someone who did not consider their life worth living, who thinks their life is pointless, would be a bit beside the point unless we could contribute in a broader way to helping them find a meaningful life. There are probably very few people like this. Most people value their lives, which is to say that they find them to be meaningful, even if they don't reflect on that fact. Nevertheless, the key point is that feeding people is not an end in itself but rather a means to allow them to live in ways they consider worth the living.

If this is right, then the point of aiding others is to contribute to their ability to live meaningful lives. But if everyone deserves to live a meaningful life, then it would seem that

I deserve to do so as well. And to ask that I sacrifice things that make my life meaningful in order to assist others in their quest for a meaningful life is actually treating my life as *less* worthy than theirs. That is to say, even if we accept that we have an important duty to assist others in desperate straits, that duty is limited to activities that will not undermine aspects of my life that make it worth living for me.

This limitation is one that still demands a lot of me. After all, there are plenty of things I do that, while enjoyable, don't have a place in conferring the meaning my life has. I could forgo a number of restaurant dinners, movie outings, fancy coffees, and other forms of entertainment while still living in a way I find to be meaningful. The point here is that, even if we accept that we have an important duty to aid those who are starving—or oppressed or marginalized or dying of preventable illnesses—this does not require that I sacrifice the central aspects of what confers significance on my life to do so. Otherwise put, there is a limit to the strictness of the morality to which I am required to submit.

This argument is what might be called *permissive*. That is to say, the importance of what makes life meaningful gives me permission to limit my aid to others. But perhaps we can go further. Perhaps we can say that living something other than an altruistic life (bearing in mind that I'm using the term *altruism* to mean adherence to a very strict morality of whatever kind) might actually be a positive good. It might, in some ways, make the world a better place, or at least a more interesting one. It may be that certain pursuits and ways of being that don't contribute to the elimination of starvation, and so on, actually make the world a better place to live in the sense of being a place with a greater variety of activities and ways of living.[14]

There are people who dedicate themselves to excelling at a sport. Think of Serena Williams or LeBron James. There are others whose passion is to paint or to write or to create music: Van Gogh, Chinua Achebe, Beethoven. Still others seek to be great lovers or dedicated parents or loyal friends. None of these activities would necessarily conform to a strict morality, and even if one did, it would do so in an odd way. Imagine Serena Williams or Beethoven striving to be good at tennis and music because it would cause the most good or conform to the categorical imperative or express virtue. The contributions they make to the world are rooted in their desire to do what they do: play sports or create art or engage with others they care about. They do not stem from an adherence to a set of moral ideals, regardless of what those ideals are.

Now imagine a world without people like this. Such a world seems impoverished. Not only would the variety of the world be eliminated, many of the activities that enhance our lives would no longer be available to us. Our lives might be morally better, but they would also be less meaningful to us. The world would be less engaging. It is precisely because there are people—including many of *us*—who are not dedicated to moral improvement but rather to some other practice that we have access to many of the things that make our lives worth our living.

This vision is not shared by people like Peter Singer. In "Famine, Affluence, and Morality," one of the examples he offers of money that could have been better used to end famine is that spent on building the Sydney Opera House. Singer might point out, rightfully, that there is something odd about contributing to the maintenance of opera when others do not have enough to eat or are dying of curable diseases. And in the individual case this is certainly true. If I have money to give, it would probably be better for me to give it to an organization that feeds the hungry—or, perhaps better, an organization that seeks to militate against a political and economic system that allows for hunger in the midst of plenty—than to the creation of an opera house. But what holds for me as an individual does not hold for all of us collectively. Let's suppose that nobody contributed to the creation of centers for music or art, that nobody dedicated themselves to sports or personal relationships or even hiking the Appalachian trail. Under those conditions, the world would be leeched of many of its hues.

It is possible that in a world like this, if everyone was solely dedicated to being an exemplary moral person, it wouldn't matter. The only thing that would matter is achieving moral ideals. However, that would be a world of moral Stepford wives, wouldn't it? The richness that our lives possess or at least have access to would be gone. To be sure, there would likely be no starvation, and that is not a little. But the projects and practices that are built upon having the basics—food, shelter, health—would not be available to us. And there's the rub.

The two arguments we have seen against a strict morality converge. The first one says that if the goal of aiding others is to make meaningful lives available to them, then I should have permission to create a meaningful life for myself as well. The second one says that if everyone acted in accordance with a strict morality, there would be less access for many of us to live a very meaningful life. Taken together, these seem to make a strong case against the relation to morality that Singer and other strict moralists propose.

I want to add a third consideration. This is a much more pedestrian one, but I believe it applies to almost all of us. It is not unrelated to the first two but is distinct from them as well. The fact is that the vast majority of us are incapable of the kind of strict morality that Singer and others endorse. Even if it were a good thing—and ending starvation would certainly be a good thing—dedicating ourselves to an extreme form of altruism is beyond us. Very few of us don't care about morality. But we are too dedicated to our nonmoral engagements to be able to drop all of them when morality seems to require it.

Think of the commitments you have that may not conform to the moral requirements of, say, consequentialism. Would much of the time you spend with your lover, your friends, or your kids not be better spent raising money for a charity that helps cure river blindness or educates people about the effects of climate change? Should I really be writing this book when I can instead visit kids with cancer in hospitals, bring them gifts, and cheer them up? And shouldn't I spend a lot more time convincing people to be vegetarians, given the cruelty to animals of factory farming and the effects of such farming on the environment? (More on this in chapters 3 and 4.) There is no doubt that I could do more good if I arranged my life in accordance with a utilitarian calculus.

What is true for consequentialism is also true in different ways for Kantian deontology and virtue ethics. Should I never favor my loved ones through small exaggerations to others about their fine points, or never fail to keep a small promise when breaking it might allow me to join my old friend who is just passing through town in watching a beautiful sunset? Or should I ensure that I am always hitting the best mean in my comportment, never being rash in my actions or unmeasured in passions?

The fact is, I am too committed to the projects of my life to sacrifice them on the altar of extreme moral altruism. This may or may not be a good thing, depending on what you think of the arguments just presented. Nevertheless, it is my reality, and, I suspect, the reality for most of us. And because of this, perhaps we need to think about what a morality for people like the rest of us might look like.

SEEKING AN ALTERNATIVE

If we are to create a moral vision based on a more realistic view of what we are morally capable of, what would it be? The arguments above, after all, may convince us that we are permitted to take account of the meaningfulness of our lives, or that it would even be better in some ways to do so, or at least that most of us can't live within the framework of a strict morality. But that doesn't offer any positive guidance regarding how we *should* take up our moral tasks, given the restrictions on morality for which they argue. Otherwise put, these arguments are largely negative in character. They don't give us an alternative framework for thinking about morality in other than altruistic terms.

The fact is, so much philosophical reflection has been dedicated to different understandings of "the good life" that a life that is less than that (or *other* than that) has received very little attention. There have been many arguments that are dedicated to showing that we need not be as morally focused as the extreme forms of these theories require. However, it is one thing to argue that we don't have to be moral altruists of one stripe or another, or at least to admit that we are not capable of it. It is quite another to say what a substantial but nonaltruistic morality might look like.

In seeking such a moral view, one obvious answer seems to impose itself at the outset. Perhaps we can take one or another of the moral views on offer and dial it back a bit to accommodate our other commitments and projects. Maybe we need not think about morality differently, but instead adopt a sort of consequentialism-lite, or deontology-lite, or virtue ethics-lite. Rather than developing an entirely different perspective, we could just dim the lights a bit on the moral theories we have in front of us and act in accordance with one of them. Wouldn't that do the trick?

In fact, this idea has already occurred among philosophers. Consider the unlovely term *satisficing*, which was introduced in the context of consequentialist theory.[15] The idea of satisficing recognizes that optimizing moral consequences of every decision is too much to ask of a person. We have seen the depth of sacrifice this would involve. However, perhaps optimization is not necessary. Instead of seeking to produce the best consequences all the time, one should dedicate one's moral energies toward producing good enough consequences, or better consequences than some of one's current life choices might otherwise produce.

In one way, this appears to be a bit of obvious advice. For most of us it seems a good thing, a morally good thing, to make the world a better place (although it is not so obvious for Kant, for whom it is intentions rather than outcomes that matter). The question is whether, in taking satisficing on board, we can now count consequentialism as a helpful theory in understanding and moving forward with our daily moral lives. Here things get complicated. As we have seen, consequentialism has its quirks. It seems to allow for kinds of moral luck that most of us would want to reject. It also has other unpalatable implications. Here's one. It would seem that consequentialism would counsel us to punish a person for a crime they did not commit in order to save two other innocent people from being punished for it.

Imagine the supervisor in the office you're working in is biased against two of your coworkers. One of the laptops has gone missing from the office, and your supervisor, without evidence, accuses these coworkers of colluding to steal the computer. Let's suppose he says that they've been talking suspiciously while looking at the laptop in question. Now you don't know who stole the laptop, or even whether it was stolen at all. But you do know that in addition to these coworkers, your supervisor doesn't like Sally. If you say that you saw Sally do it, the boss will fire her and it will save the jobs of your other two coworkers.

In this case, consequentialism, at least in its traditional form, would recommend that you accuse Sally. It would not simply say that it is okay to accuse Sally; it would say you *should* do it. That would be the best thing to do, the morally right thing, since it would save the jobs of several other coworkers, who are likely just as innocent as Sally is. As with the cases of moral luck we looked at, this seems an unacceptable way to conduct our moral lives.[16]

Not all types of consequentialism would counsel accusing Sally,[17] although most would allow for some forms of moral luck (although perhaps not the most offensive examples). So perhaps it would be possible to construct a consequentialist moral theory that would incorporate satisficing. It would be fairly complicated, since it would have to provide theoretical ways around some of consequentialism's traditional difficulties. In addition, it would have to tell us something about how much in the way of good consequences is enough. After all, almost everyone will agree that consequences matter. And most of us will not be able to live in such a way as to seek to create the best consequences all the time. In that sense, we're all "satisficers." But if we are to have guidance from a consequentialist moral theory, then it's going to have to say something about when we've reached the satisficing level. Adding that challenge alongside the others will make for a fairly complicated theory.

I do not want to say this cannot be done. My worry is different. Even if it can be done—and it is certainly worth attempting—then it is not clear how helpful it would be in assisting us in our daily moral lives. Such a theory would in all likelihood need to be constructed at a fairly abstract level. (When I say abstract here, I don't mean difficult, but rather abstracted or distant from mundane moral practice.) So in addition to the theory there would have to be ways to say how the theory is to be applied to our moral lives. And at that point we might be tempted by another question. Might there be another way of approaching our daily moral lives that does not need first to ascend to an abstract moral theory? Could we not construct a different frame for thinking morally, one that recognizes our moral limits and yet offers us some guidance without being as divorced from our moral practice as consequentialist theory?

This is not to say that there is no use for such an abstract theory. There are moral dilemmas that might be difficult to navigate from within a moral framework that is focused on daily living. To anticipate, the framework I will offer here will be unable to solve some serious moral dilemmas. In cases like that, having a more rigorous moral theory to appeal to would be helpful. However, it is the wager of this book that there is at least one way of framing our moral lives that, from within the moral limits of most of us, can help us recognize what we often do and yet guide us in our commonplace moral lives. And that framework does not require an abstract moral theory.

However, if consequentialism won't help us live within our moral limits, perhaps deontology or virtue ethics will. In fact, deontology, especially in its Kantian version, is even less promising than consequentialism. With consequentialism, we at least have a rough idea of what it means to satisfice, that is, to do less than try to maximize the good. This is because consequentialism is about amounts, specifically amounts of good. If we are really good consequentialists, we will produce the most amount of good we can. If we are satisficers, we'll produce less. Kantian deontology, in many cases (although admittedly not all), doesn't have a concept of the more and the less, and so it is unclear how we are to go about being less than fully deontological.[18] Does this mean that we don't keep our promises all the time, or that we lie periodically? Does it mean that I act in accordance with the categorical imperative 70 percent of the time instead of 100 percent? It is difficult to get a grip on what a Kantian deontology would look like in a more modest form.

Perhaps we can approach the categorical imperative in another way. Surely we cannot live up to the categorical imperative all the time. It is too much to be always honest, to keep all our promises, to help others whenever the opportunity arises, to develop our talents to the best of our abilities. However, we can hold up the categorical imperative as a model of how we should act, and seek to live up to it as best we can. We can take it as an ideal by which we can measure our own moral conduct and our moral progress. We may never achieve this ideal in full—in fact, most of us probably won't—but at least we will have some guidance about what we ought to aspire to. Otherwise put, we will all be moral failures, but perhaps some of us will fail less egregiously than others.

There are problems even with this view. As we have already seen, Kantian deontology does have its quirks. Should I really aspire to keep all my promises even in situations where it could cause me to ignore a great harm that I can prevent? Should I seek not to lie even when telling the truth will only serve to hurt someone's feelings? If Kantian deontology is going to be an adequate moral guide, then it will need to be revised in ways that make it more responsive to the dilemmas of daily moral practice. But then we run the risk, as many people have noted, of a categorical imperative whose principles are determined by our experience rather than being a guide to it. Can we instead construct a moral framework that would be more useful in thinking about our mundane moral lives? In constructing this moral framework we need not neglect the core idea of many deontological views, that intention matters. But neither do we need to place intention at its center and seek to characterize all moral action in terms of it.

How about virtue ethics? In some ways this seems more promising than the other two views. We can be more or less brave or magnanimous or (to use more modern virtues) patient or tolerant. In a way, it may seem that Aristotle and his contemporary followers have offered us a moral view that can admit of the more and the less, and so can offer guidance to those of us who are not likely to embody full virtue but seek to be morally decent. And this way of taking things would not be entirely beside the point.

There is a limitation here. Virtue ethics asks us to develop particular virtues, virtues that have a broadly moral character. We might think of these virtues as themes for our lives. Recall that for Aristotle the good life is not to be assessed by its particular acts in the way that consequentialism and Kantian deontology do. Rather, it should be assessed on personal character, on the themes that characterize that life. Virtue ethics proposes a set of themes (or different sets of themes, depending on the virtue ethicist) that properly characterize a good life. And, if we are interested in morality, that good life should be a morally good one.

However, there are other themes that might be said to characterize a life that would give it meaning but not be considered specifically moral themes.[19] Some lives might be characterized by themes of intensity or curiosity. Other lives express themes of spirituality or steadfastness or spontaneity. And these themes may be central in making the life a significant one for the person living it. Imagine certain rock singers (in my generation, Jimi Hendrix, Janis Joplin, James Brown) without intensity animating their lives. Consider friends you know whose spontaneity inspires you, or whose spirituality— even if you don't share it—is a source of admiration. These nonmoral themes are often central in making a life worthwhile for those who live it and inspiring for those who come across it. We would not, however, call these themes virtues, but rather something more like narrative values of meaning for those who live them.

Moreover, it can be that these narrative values come into conflict with moral virtues. The spontaneous person may neglect some moral obligations, or the spontaneous person may drift away from previous commitments, leaving others in the lurch. It has been asked of Aristotle's view whether all the virtues are necessarily convergent or mutually supporting in the way he believed them to be. When we look at other values, however, we have a deeper problem. Not only are some values not mutually supporting; they can be in open conflict. In cases like this, we might need to sacrifice some of the fullness of a virtue in order to accommodate other values that contribute to the meaningfulness of our lives.

This does not require us to be entirely unvirtuous. We need not abandon all moral integrity for the sake of other values. Rather, it may be that in order for a person's life to be meaningful to them, they cannot simply follow the virtuous path but instead must veer off at point onto other paths, paths without which they would not recognize their life as *theirs*. The parent who is steadfastly loyal to the daughter who brings light to her world cannot be expected to act with moral probity, or even with honesty, if the daughter is rightfully accused of something whose punishment would bring her great harm. Nor can what Aristotle calls temperance be asked of someone who throws their life into an artistic endeavor, convinced that only through committing their entire self to their art can they make it succeed. We need not entirely admire people like this. But neither need we—and we often do not—entirely fault them either. If their lapse is a moral one, it is also one that is both understandable and perhaps, in a way that is nonmoral, laudable as well.

None of the three traditional moral views we have canvassed here seems capable, without significant revision, of accommodating the fact that most of us will not, indeed cannot, live entirely moral lives. We are something less—or perhaps something other—than altruists. Our lives involve projects and commitments whose importance to us may conflict at points with moral requirements. And at times we simply are not up to the task. We want to be moral beings, but for a variety of reasons, and for better or worse, our lives get in the way. Is there a manner of approaching morality that can both allow us our lives and at the same time give us a sense of how to proceed morally? Can we discover or construct a framework that recognizes our moral limits yet gives us moral guidance, a framework that perhaps cannot help us through deep moral dilemmas but can offer assistance in our daily engagements?

We might be tempted by a simple approach, one that elim-
inates the necessity of constructing a moral framework. Perhaps we can just have a list of duties that would suffice for
minimal moral decency. Follow the rules and you're a morally decent person. Perhaps not morally great, but at least
decent. Would a set of rules to follow provide us with the
material we need to conduct our lives in ways that while not
altruistic are at least morally acceptable to us?

We might fear, indeed I think we should fear, that such a
list would not offer moral decency but probably something
more like moral mediocrity. After all, most of us are not
simply interested in performing our basic moral duties and
then moving on. We seek to integrate morality into our lives,
to make it part of who we are. We would like the threads of
our moral existence to be woven into the larger fabric of our
lives, even though we acknowledge that not all the moral
threads will fit the weave. We want morality to be an issue for
us as we navigate through the world, not simply an external
demand placed upon us.[20]

HOW SHALL WE PROCEED?

It seems, then, that for those of us who want a helpful moral
framework for our daily lives, we cannot rely on traditional
moral theories either in their rigorous or slightly watered
down form, nor can we appeal straightforwardly to the concept of moral duties. We must look elsewhere. What this
book proposes is a different frame for moral reflection. It
starts from the premise that most of us would like to be
moral but that we will not or cannot be moral altruists. Its
goal is to provide a way of thinking that not only helps us
see what we already do morally but allows us to further our
moral behavior in ways that remain within the parameters of

what we can reasonably ask of ourselves. If this framework is to be helpful, both of these challenges must be met. If we only meet the first one—telling us what we already do—there would be no need for a framework. It might be nice to have one, but it wouldn't offer us any guidance for our further moral action. "Oh, so that's how we act. Cool," would probably be the best response to a framework like that. And if we only meet the second one—giving us guidance—the proposed moral framework would not hook on to our current moral behavior. It wouldn't give us a way of moving forward *from where we are*. It runs the risk of feeling alien to us. So it will have to perform both tasks at once.

It would be helpful, I think (I hope!) to locate this framework somewhere in between the abstractness of traditional moral theories and the specific types of moral acts we perform: more general than the latter, less general than the former. It will certainly borrow from the intuitions of traditional moral theories. After all, for most of us, consequences, intentions, and being a generally good person all matter morally. But it will not seek to decide among them in favor of one or another. In this way, the view offered here will be a little more diverse, or perhaps even more scattered, than traditional moral theories.

However, there will be a single guiding thought that runs throughout. It is one that is not uncommon among moral philosophers. For many, in fact, it is the central theme of morality.[21] This is the idea that decent moral action recognizes that there are others in the world who have lives to live. The idea lies at the heart of what I am calling "decency." With regard to human beings (who will not be our only concern here), I have elsewhere elaborated the idea this way: "We have a sense of what it is in general to lead a human life: to engage in projects and relationships that unfold over time; to be aware of one's death in a way that affects how one sees the arc of one's life; to have biological needs like food, shelter, and sleep; to have basic psychological needs like care and a sense of attachment to one's surroundings."[22] This is not meant to be an exhaustive definition of what it is to live a human life but rather a gesture in the right direction to help guide us in our behavior toward one another.

But we must be clear at the outset. To say that others have lives to live, and even to admit that their lives are no less valuable than mine, that my life is only one among others, is not to say that I am committed to treating all those lives on an equal moral plane. That thought, which is in line with both consequentialism and deontology, leads us back to the kind of extreme altruism of which most of us are not capable. If we are to treat everyone else as being on an equal moral plane with ourselves and those we care for, then it is possible that we would have to sacrifice our interests—and perhaps our most significant interests—when they are outweighed by the interests of others, even distant others. This is the territory occupied by Peter Singer and those who are allied with him. Perhaps it is possible, however, to recognize that others have lives to live and to respect that fact without having to embrace the conclusion that I must treat the interests of those lives as equal to my own. Or, even if morally I am *obliged* to treat those interests as equal, perhaps I can conduct myself in a way that does not fully meet my obligations but that still takes those others into account.

This might strike some as moral mediocrity. What decency is there in not living up to one's moral obligations? How can I call myself a decent person if I am not acting on the fundamental moral idea that the interests of all are equal?

As Singer points out in his essay on famine and affluence, the idea that "if it is in our power to prevent something bad from happening, without sacrificing anything of comparable moral importance, we ought, morally, to do it" is "uncontroversial."[23] By "uncontroversial" he does not mean easy. In fact, the point of the essay is to educate us about how difficult the requirements flowing from it would be. Rather, it is uncontroversial as a moral principle, since it relies on the idea that the interests of all are equal.

And, indeed, from Singer's point of view, what this book proposes is likely some form of moral mediocrity. I do not share that point of view. It seems to me one thing to say that the ideal moral standard would have us act altruistically. It is quite another to say that anything that does not measure up to that standard is less than morally decent. I have insisted that while most of us are not capable of living up to the moral standards proposed by traditional moral theories, we would like our lives to take place within a broadly moral framework. (And, as we have seen, it is even an open question of whether everyone should always act morally.) To the extent that this is true, it raises the question of what that moral framework would look like.

My suggestion is that we can construct a moral framework starting from the recognition that others have lives to lead and a general idea of what that means without having to embrace in our conduct the conclusion of traditional moral theory that we must treat the interests of those other lives as equal to our own. This leaves the question of how we are supposed to conduct ourselves in regard to that recognition a bit vague. That, in itself, should not be troubling. Although the rest of this book is dedicated to putting flesh on that idea, we should not ask for more precision than can be supplied.

As Aristotle—often wise when he wasn't being misogynist or racist—reminds us in his *Nichomachean Ethics*, "the educated person seeks exactness in each area to the extent that the nature of the subject allows; for apparently it is just as mistaken to demand demonstrations from a rhetorician as to accept merely persuasive arguments from a mathematician."[24] The goal then will be to construct a moral framework for the rest of us who are not altruists that offers as much exactness as the nature of the subject allows.

In constructing this framework, I will start close to home and then work my way outward in several directions. That is to say, I will begin by asking about our moral relations with those with whom we come into interpersonal contact. These include not only our friends and family, but also strangers we run across in our daily lives. It may also include people with whom we have virtual contact through email and particularly through media such as Skype or Facetime. Then we will turn to those more distant from us in both space and time. From there we can look at others who are more distant from us in a different way: nonhuman animals. Finally, we will ask what the framework that has emerged means for our political relations. Morality and politics are, after all, inseparable. Although this book starts from the moral side of things, it would seem to spin in some kind of social void if the relationships between this framework and our political lives were not brought into the picture.[25]

A final note. I don't take myself here to be offering *the* way a moral framework should be constructed when we recognize that most of us are creatures who seek to be generally moral but not altruistic. What I am seeking here is simply *one* way to construct that framework. There may be others. Moral philosophy has for too long spent itself on creating theoretical frameworks that are distant from our lives, through abstraction or through the creation of altruistic moral theories or, more often, both. Recently, that distance has been challenged, but little work has been done to offer alternative frameworks that offer general moral guidance. (The exception here is in the field that is often called "practical ethics," where much work has been done on issues like animal rights, the environment, war, abortion, and medical and business ethics. We will see some of these more specific issues in the following chapters.) The challenges themselves remain abstract. There is much to learn both from traditional moral philosophy and from its challenges. These pages could not have been written without them.

The wager of this book, however, is that a moral framework that is both enlightening and guiding can be written for those of us who want to reflect on our moral lives as nonaltruists. But the wager is a limited one. Even if it is won, there are other wagers of the same type that could be won through the construction of other moral frameworks. Indeed, there could well be others (and likely will be) that surpass this one in clarity or rigor or helpfulness. Consider this, then, an opening word and an invitation to conversation as well as reflection. We all—or almost all—are attempting to live decently. My hope is to contribute within the limits of my own abilities to one understanding of what that attempt might amount to.

DECENCY TOWARD THOSE AROUND US

In the fall semester of 2011, Matthew Stevenson, an orthodox
Jew, invited a fellow student at his college, New College in
Florida, to join him for his Friday evening Shabbat dinner.
The student's name was Derek Black. Black was not Jewish.
Normally this would not seem to be an unusual invitation.
Stevenson was the only orthodox Jew at New College, and so
his Shabbat dinner was often attended by non-Jews. However,
in this case it was very unusual. Derek Black is the son of Don
Black, a virulent white nationalist and founder of the website
Stormfront. Black had followed in his father's footsteps and
was at the time a rising star in white nationalist circles. He
had written posts on the Stormfront website that contained
such sentences as "Jews are NOT white," and "They must go."[1]
   Matthew Stevenson knew all this when he invited Black
to Shabbat dinner. He thought to himself, "Maybe he's never
spent much time with a Jewish person before." This particular
dinner was boycotted by most of the usual attendees. But it
went off well. Black brought a bottle of wine. The issues that
would have driven a wedge between him and the other participants were not discussed. Black became a regular member

of the Shabbat dinners, and gradually the other members drifted back. In the meantime, Stevenson and Black became closer, occasionally playing pool together.

What Stevenson did not know is that he was a central figure in the growing doubts Black was having about his white nationalism. Those doubts were seeded when Black began to attend New College, a liberal arts school with a diverse student body. But before he met Stevenson the effect of his new colleagues had been only to motivate him to hide his convictions rather than state them openly. Later, in good part under the influence of the Shabbat dinners, he began to question his views more deeply. Eventually he renounced his white nationalism and decided to work against it.[2]

What Matthew Stevenson did was quietly courageous. By extending an invitation to Shabbat dinner to someone who had espoused an egregiously racist and anti-Semitic philosophy, he risked at the same time the opprobrium of his friends and humiliation at the hands of a sworn enemy. And yet he recognized that Derek Black was also a person, and perhaps one who had more sides to him than Black himself might have recognized. In doing something that Black, at least in his more active political phase, would never have done for Stevenson, he acknowledged Derek Black as fully human, with a life to live like everyone else, and he acted on that recognition. And he did more than that. He went out of his way to act on that recognition, even in the face of the denial of Black's mutual recognition. He risked his own friendships and perhaps even public shame. But he did so in the name of the acknowledgment of Derek Black as a fellow human being. "Maybe he's never spent much time with a Jewish person before."

Although very different in character and far more courageous, Matthew Stevenson's invitation has something in common with the Copenhagen train riders I mentioned at the outset. In both cases, the actors treated those around them with what I am calling decency. They recognized that others have lives they are trying to live and they sought to act on that recognition. Moreover, they did so in situations where they shared a space and a time. Matthew Stevenson might not have seen Derek Black before, but they attended the same college and by the time of the initial invitation Stevenson knew a good bit about Black. Alternatively, the riders on the Copenhagen metro did not know the names of any of their fellow passengers, but they were there among them. They could see their faces, their clothing, their style of walking.

This chapter is about decency toward those with whom we broadly share a space and time. I say broadly because the limits of this sharing are difficult to draw. The Copenhagen metro riders certainly shared a time and space with their fellow riders. Matthew Stevenson attended the same college as Derek Black at the same time, but perhaps with an effort might not have met him face-to-face. We all have certain colleagues with whom we have extended email contact before we meet them, perhaps even before we know what they look like. Does this constitute sharing a time and space? Sometimes advertisements for fund-raising efforts for impoverished children present us with a child's face and even their name. How does this compare with the email contact whose face I have never seen?

For the purposes of this chapter, the email contact will count as sharing a space and time and the impoverished child will not. This, admittedly, is a difficult line to draw. The difference here is that I have interpersonal interaction with my email colleague but do not with the child (and Stevenson, for his part, was sharing a campus with Black before he met him). I bring my colleague into my space and time, and vice versa. While the Copenhagen metro riders find themselves sharing a space and time with other riders, my email contact creates a common space and time. For reasons that I hope to become clear as this chapter unfolds, that will count as being among "those around us" to whom we should be decent.

FACE-TO-FACE

In approaching this issue, let's start simply and look at interactions with those with whom we uncontroversially share space and time. We often call these interactions "face-to-face." Although that phrase is used to contrast interactions that involve people who occupy the same time and physical space with those who don't—say people on email, Skype, or in other times writing letters to each other—we should linger over the fact that these interactions give us access to the living face of one another. It is easy to pass over the fact that in these interactions a person has available to them the visage of another person, or perhaps several other persons.[3]

Recall times when you gazed into the face of someone you care for: a friend, a lover, a child. That gazing was probably characterized by affection. You seemed to see their whole being reflected in the depth of their eyes or in the roundness of their cheeks or in the way their smile lit up their features or the way they cocked their head to the side when someone else spoke to them. A whole living person appeared in front of you in all their promise and vulnerability. At moments their history with you can seem to be etched into their visage.

We too often neglect this simple experience, although it is often available to us. But when we do experience it, it is with a tenderness that emerges from a sense that we have a real life in front of us. After all, it is a life we already care about. But how often does that caring become salient for us? When we gaze actively into the face of another person that we care about, then, among other times, their life in its fullness is right there in front of us.

To recognize the importance of this experience, remember the last time you were angry with someone you love. If you shouted at them, did you at the same time gaze at their face, take it in? Of course, when you shouted, you probably did so to their face or at their face. But did you see their face as you shouted? When we shout at people there is a blurring of the features of the object of our anger. They don't appear to us in the way of someone with another life but instead as someone more anonymous. In that sense rather being engaged with the object of our anger we are instead engaged with ourselves, and specifically with the anger itself.

We can see this phenomenon especially when a parent shouts at a small child for misbehaving. (I have heard about this phenomenon. I assure you, though, that I have never done anything like this myself. No, sir. Far be it from me.) If the child starts to cry, the parent might start to feel bad; it's as though the child's full being starts to come back into view. But if the parent is too caught up in anger, that feeling gets buried under the anger, which remains the parent's focus.

Even when we do not shout at another, or after we are done shouting, we avoid gazing into the face of someone with whom we are angry. We do not meet their look. If we are living with that person a certain awkwardness takes hold of the interactions as gazes cross one another without meeting.

Usually it is only after reconciliation of the anger that gazing into the face of another is a real possibility again.

It is not surprising, then, to find that it is difficult to train people to kill others, for instance in face-to-face combat. As the philosopher John Protevi tells us, "the vast majority of soldiers cannot kill in cold blood and need to kill in a de-subjectified state, for example, in reflexes, rages, and panics." Therefore, "The military problem of the berserker rage is how to turn it on and off on command (and only on command): this is the problem of the conversion of the warrior (whose triggers include insults to honor) into the soldier who kills only on command."[4]

This is not to say that we should never be angry with another person. Others might merit our anger at certain points in our lives, as we merit the anger of others. What I am pointing to here is an experience, one that is mundane enough that it might elude reflection. In it, we come into intimate contact with the fact of a living person. Earlier I said that to lead a human life is "to engage in projects and relationships that unfold over time; to be aware of one's death in a way that affects how one sees the arc of one's life; to have biological needs like food, shelter, and sleep; to have basic psychological needs like care and a sense of attachment to one's surroundings." A recognition of the other when gazing at their face is an arresting awareness of something like this.

Of course, we don't tell ourselves this. We don't say to ourselves, "My goodness, here is someone engaged in projects and relationships, and so on." Our experience of another person when gazing at their face is not reflective in this way. We might put the point by saying that in gazing at the face of another what we do instead is have a sense of the fullness of a life, one that, if we reflected on it, we would recognize as being engaged with projects and relationships, and so on. In the immediate experience we are gripped by the life itself in a way that is beneath or beyond our cognitive grip.

We have been talking here of people we know: friends and family. However, the idea can be extended. We often don't think about this because we often don't gaze at the face of our colleagues or strangers in the same way that we do with those we know. We don't take them in visually. Our gaze doesn't linger; it glances off them and fastens on something else. However, if we watch someone we know only casually, say when they are sitting across from us in our office, we can elicit the experience of sensing their life in their face.

It can happen elsewhere as well. I recall once walking on a cold winter night in New York. I passed someone standing in a doorway who asked me whether I had some spare change. I handed him some without thinking much about him and then continued on my way. About half a block later I passed by another man sitting against a wall. He too asked me whether I could spare a little money. I figured he wasn't in a strategically well-placed spot, so I said as I passed him (without looking at him), "I'm sorry, there's a guy a half a block back that I just gave some money to." He responded with a smile in his voice (who forgets things like this?), "Yeah, well I'm an independent operator." At that point I turned to look at him and saw someone with a real face smiling at me. We talked a few minutes about the cold and I gave him some money. As I look back on it, the idea of his being an independent operator suggests metaphorically the underlying thought of this book. We are all independent operators in the sense that we are all people with our own lives to lead, lives whose value is not dependent on the acknowledgement of others. (In another sense we aren't so independent. More on that below.)

It is actually difficult to look at the face of someone begging for money and then walk past them indifferently. This, however, is precisely the kind of simple recommendation urged by the great homeless activist Mitch Snyder. During the Reagan administration, Snyder went on a hunger strike to pressure the President and Congress to devote funds to renovating an abandoned building his group, the Center for Creative Nonviolence, had turned into a homeless shelter. After the administration agreed to fund the renovation but neglected to turn over funds, Snyder embarked on a second, waterless fast (which allows one to survive only about a week or so) to get the funds, which finally the administration released.[5] While Snyder himself was an altruist of the first order, his advice to the rest of us was simple: look at a homeless person as though they were another human being. Don't just walk by. He knew that that first act of meeting the gaze of another would elicit a human reaction that would place the homeless person on another plane in relation to us. Rather than being an object to avoid, the person would be another human being to be interacted with.

Of course, in a large urban center it is difficult to look every homeless person in the face. Imagine doing this in Kolkata, or even New York. However, the exercise of looking here and there into the face of another, particularly another whom one is tempted to treat indifferently, can bring the humanity of that person into view, the fact that they too have a life they are struggling to live. I suspect such an exercise not only brings their humanity into view more clearly but also elevates our own just a bit.

You will immediately recognize what I mentioned above: the practice of those who solicit money for charity using advertisements with faces on them, usually the faces of children. Although I have no empirical evidence for this, I'm quite sure those ads are more effective than would be ads that merely told us how many people were suffering from a particular disease or impoverishment.

The faces of people around us, when we let ourselves look at them, can reveal on a visceral level the fact that they have lives to live, which is the motivating idea of the framework I am seeking to construct here. It can move us to treat others in more humane ways than we might otherwise be tempted to. This "otherwise" isn't necessarily a matter of competing with our self-interest. Rather it is because we simply don't see (literally do not see) their lives in front of us. Caught up in our own projects, we are not gripped by the fact of another person's existence. To be gripped by the existence of other people's lives, however, does not imply that we need to treat those lives with the same solicitude as we treat our own or those we care deeply about. The goal rather would be to develop as best we can a certain sensitivity, one that is based on a phenomenon we can recognize: the role of the face of others in revealing the fact of their living to us.

Seeing the face of another person, being confronted with it or gripped by it, places the life of another person before us. In different situations it might lead us to different courses of action. My anger at someone who has kept me waiting softens when I look into the face of the person arriving and see pensiveness that might indicate a troubled mind, or joy to see me, or just the face of someone I have come to care about. My indifference toward the person crowded next to me on a train during rush hour might, if I see their face, move

me to offer them another few inches of space or help clear
the way for them if they've reached their stop. Looking into
the face of the cashier at the supermarket might lead me to
smile at them in a more sincere way than I would have if I
had, as I usually do, just looked through them, seeing only
my own life.

COMMON DECENCY

In engaging with those around us we need not always be cognizant of their lives. We can have more informal contact with
others, contact that often goes by the name of "common decency." Here are a few situations of common decency: helping an older person across the street, lighting a cigarette for
a stranger, holding the door for someone you don't know,
or motioning to someone looking for a parking space that
you're about to get into your car to leave, or placing a napkin
over someone's cup of coffee to keep it warm when they get
up to go to the bathroom during a meeting.[6] These are things
we do for people, or might do for them, even if we don't know
them, even if we will never see them again. These are forms
of politeness that are specific to particular societies. Other
societies have other forms, for instance Japanese culture encourages the giving of gifts, and often nicer gifts, in a wider
set of social circumstances than usually occurs among Americans. There are, in different cultures, different patterns of
common decency, and often these are ritualized so as to be
recognized by their recipients. As the ancient Chinese philosopher Confucius recognized, there is a deep bond between
rituals like these and the preservation of social peace. In the
Analects he insists, "In the uses of ritual it is harmony that
is prized. . . . If harmony itself is not modulated by ritual,
things will still go amiss."[7] These rituals are all ways of being

with others that create minimal bonds among strangers.[8] To act with common decency is to do something for a stranger or someone one does not know well that makes their following moments a little bit more pleasant.

Acts of common decency like these assume that we recognize the existence of the other people, and not merely their existence. It is to recognize that another person is carrying on a life and that we can do something to make that carrying on just a wee bit less complicated. It is a way of brightening a life. It can also be contagious, and in a couple of ways. First, a person who has been the recipient of an act of common decency is often motivated to pay it forward. It's as though common decency presents a model for the recipient to follow in the next stages of their unfolding day. That model may not last long. It may last only until the next person they encounter acts like a jerk. Nevertheless, it has the potential to be passed from one person to another.

Common decency can also be contagious in another way. It can stand as a model not just for the recipient of the act of decency but also for those who witness it. I am sure I am not the only person who has noticed that when someone drops a coin into a charity box or leaves a tip at a coffee counter or holds the door for someone, those who see it are more likely to do it in their turn. Once, when I was waiting for a meeting on a college campus, I looked out the window at two students who were leafletting. It was striking to me that when one person took an offered leaflet the others who immediately followed her were more likely to do so, and when someone walked by without taking the leaflet others were more likely to follow suit. Of course, this wasn't universally true, or else either everyone or no one would have taken the leaflets. Rather, each person either taking or refusing seemed to raise the probability that the next person would do the same. In our public actions we often model, give permission, encourage or discourage others to follow suit.

One of the most infamous examples of this is in the Milgram experiments.⁹ Stanley Milgram, under the pretense of seeking to understand the role of negative reinforcement on learning behavior, conducted experiments which seemed to show that people were willing to engage in egregious acts of shocking others to encourage them to learn if an authority figure were there encouraging to administer the shock. However, in one of the variations on the experiment, there was also another person in the room with the subject who refused to "shock" the "learner." Milgram found that his subjects were more likely to refuse to follow orders when another person also did so.

What often goes under the heading of common decency works like that, except in a positive direction. It can encourage such decency among those who receive it and those who witness it. And, although it can emerge from or be accompanied by an encounter with the face of someone else, it need not. I can put my napkin over someone's cup of coffee even if I have wandered into a meeting with strangers thinking about something else and not really noticing who is around me.

It would be going too far to say that common decency is always contagious. It isn't even always acknowledged by its recipients. We all know of situations like this. You hold the door for someone who then walks through it as though you don't exist. You smile and thank a cashier who looks like they could use a smile, but they don't look at you and instead just call out, "Next." You offer to help someone carry a large package down a flight of steps; they snap back, "I can carry it myself!" What is happening in all these cases? You are being disrespected as a person. It is as though, for these people whom you are offering to assist briefly in their lives, you are simply an object. You are not being recognized as another person. It isn't always that you want to be thanked or treated as some kind of hero of common decency. (Okay, there might be a tinge of that. But most of the time it probably isn't the dominant desire.) Rather, you simply want your gesture to be acknowledged as coming from someone. Often, a perfunctory smile in return for your offer will do. Sometimes, though, your existence is entirely ignored, or even affronted.

When this happens, it stings. The immediate response can be a sense of rejection or anger. It's as though we want to re-establish ourselves as mattering in the wake of being dismissed. And re-establishing ourselves (particularly if we are male) often takes the form of wanting to place the other person beneath us, denying them as a person with a life, making them feel smaller. It is often difficult at these moments to say to ourselves that the person walking through the door may just be distracted or taken up with a personal concern, that being a cashier and having to smile at a zillion customers is a daily burden, that the person who snaps at the offer of help may be trying to prove to themselves that they're not getting too old to carry large packages, or perhaps their back, sore from lugging packages around, is making them cranky. The failure to acknowledge common decency may not have its source in disrespect but instead in the strains or even mundane self-involvement of those we offer it to.

This isn't always the case. As we all know from unpleasant experience, sometimes people can be, well, as the philosopher Aaron James has put it in technical terms, assholes. In his book of the same name, he tells us that "a person counts as an *asshole* when, and only when, he systematically allows himself to enjoy special advantages in interpersonal relations out of an entrenched sense of entitlement that immunizes him against the complaints of other people."[10] (He notes that the use of the male pronoun is deliberate.) Such a person not only rarely offers common decency to others, but rarely acknowledges the common decency offered to them. They take it as their due. For James, the difference between an asshole and a psychopath is that morality plays no role for the psychopath whereas the asshole possesses a keen sense of moral entitlement. Moreover, and this is where James's view intersects with our concerns, what drives people crazy about an asshole is that "he fails to recognize others in a fundamental, morally important way."[11] For the asshole, other people's existence, their lives and their plans, do not matter because the only thing that matters is his life. Therefore, there is no need to offer or even notice common decency, since he is the center of the universe.

It takes a good degree of self-acceptance to maintain a recognition of the person whose behavior in the face of common decency is disrespectful. However, perhaps that self-acceptance can be a worthy goal. Or perhaps things can go the other way around: by maintaining a recognition of the other person as having a life to live, one that may preoccupy them in ways that we are not privy to, we come to accept ourselves a little more than we had previously. We achieve a little more balance.

On the other end of things, common decency can extend itself beyond the small acts of kindness we do for others. Where one draws the line between decency and a more extreme altruism is a difficult question. Was Matthew Stevenson's Shabbat invitation to Derek Black an example of decency or of altruism? It certainly wasn't a profound act of self-denial. On the other hand, it wasn't simply a matter of covering a cup of coffee with a napkin or, Japanese-style, bringing a nice gift to the home of someone you don't know well. Stevenson risked alienating his traditional Shabbat partners, and in fact did alienate them for a little while. For our purposes there is no need to draw a bright line between common decency and altruism. What we are after instead is an understanding of our general moral relations with those around us, an understanding that can both tell us what we are about morally and can offer reasonable paths to extend what we are about.

This understanding, we can see, contrasts with the altruism characteristic of the moral theories we canvassed in the previous chapter. In being moved by the faces of those around us and in engaging in common decency we do not seek to maximize the consequences of our actions. Nor do we hope to act as a moral exemplar in accordance with the categorical imperative. Although we may, in displaying decency, mold ourselves into slightly better people, we need not be guided by a model of virtue. Decency (not just common decency but decency more broadly) in the sense that I am trying to develop it is not a matter of making the world as good a place as we can make it or of living the best life for human beings. But neither is it a matter of meeting some set of minimal moral obligations. Instead, it is a matter of recognizing others as having lives to live and seeking to incorporate that recognition into our lives in ways that are reasonably workable, or, to put it in a more positive light, to navigate through the world with a certain moral gracefulness.

I would like to linger over the idea of moral gracefulness for a moment, since it offers us a way of thinking about our moral lives that is more positive than some other ways we are encouraged to think about them. Often morality is characterized in terms of duties and obligations. It is thought to be a matter of what we owe to one another. This characterization, in turn, is grounded in the idea that there is a moral bottom line in our relations to one another that is important to recognize. Kant was keen on duties and obligations, and utilitarianism, although it uses different terms, is also committed to the idea that we are obliged to create the most good we can. More recently, many theories that are called social contract theories ask the question of what rules we would commit ourselves to follow if we could be assured that others would also follow the same rules.[12]

If we think in these terms we are likely to bring in ideas of debt and then guilt in their wake. Where there is obligation, there is debt; and where there is debt, a failure to pay the debt leads to guilt, perhaps even to shame. Guilt can be thought of in psychological terms, but we should also recognize the legal connotation of the word. An obligation is like a law someone must follow, a law that levies a debt on someone. If you don't pay the debt levied by the obligation, then you are guilty of not meeting your obligations. Thinking of morality in these terms is very contractual.

It also sets up morality as a burden to be borne. No doubt there is something to this. If there weren't, it wouldn't have been the framework of moral thought for so many great philosophers over the past centuries. Morality can be a burden, as when I am asked to act in ways that I would prefer not to because there is a moral reason to do so. And in difficult situations I may be asked to do precisely that. However, there is another way to think about how we steer ourselves through the world morally in most of our daily interactions with others, one that focuses less on our duties and obligations and more on what we can offer. That way of thinking is more pull than push. When I see the face of another, really *see* it, I am driven to acknowledge that person not so much through a sense of burden but through what might better be called commonality or solidarity or kindness (if we keep in mind the connotation of being of like kind). This other person grips me not as a duty to be discharged but as a fellow person sharing the world with me, someone whom I am drawn to recognize and perhaps to assist. To say that this recognition is a joy rather than a burden would in most cases probably be claiming too much. It is probably more accurate to say that there is a felt bond with this person that moves me toward them, that draws my attention in their direction.

Although common decency need not have the same grip or emerge from the same bond—since it isn't necessarily stirred by someone's face—neither must we think of it in most cases as a burden. It seems rather to be an opportunity for solidarity with another person, often a stranger. Smiling at others, holding doors for them, assisting them in minor ways when they are in difficulty, or giving them small gifts is a way of sharing the world with someone, often someone you don't know. We are not alone on the planet, and we need not act as though we were alone (well, except perhaps for assholes). And our way of not being alone need not be characterized in legalistic terms of obligations and debts, rather in more positive terms of sharing and recognition. Common decency seems to me better understood in those latter terms. And by this I mean not only that it can be understood that way but more strongly that it probably *is* understood that way by most people who exercise common decency.

Peter Singer, the promoter of altruism we met in the first chapter, believes that many altruists are motivated not by a sense of guilt or shame but instead by the positive feeling of offering themselves to others. In his book *The Most Good You Can Do*, he cites examples of people whose lives are enhanced by their dedication to charitable giving. He notes studies that show that charitable giving and even donating organs can lead to more happiness and that giving enhances the important good of self-esteem. "The most solid basis for self-esteem," he writes, "is to live an ethical life, that is, a life in which one contributes to the greatest possible extent to making the world a better place."[13]

There is a core idea here that I would like to hold on to: acting morally can often arise out of a positive sense of contribution rather than a negative one of guilt or indebtedness. However, the examples he uses—of organ donations to strangers and of people calculating how much good their resources can do and living largely if not solely by those calculations—are difficult for most of us to follow. Of course, we might ask, as we did in the first chapter, whether the world would actually be a better place if everyone lived that way, if nobody followed their passions for artistic creation, rock climbing, spontaneity, or love. But even if we thought that it would be better if we all threw ourselves into what Singer calls "effective altruism," the fact is that most of us are not going to do this. (I assume I am not alone here, am I?)

This does not mean, however, that the giving we do, through what the faces of others or common decency moves us to do (or in other ways that we will see in later chapters), cannot be done with a positive feeling, a sense that comes out of our bonds with others rather than our desire to be quits with morality.

But why is this important? Why the emphasis on bonds with others rather than a more legalistic relation to morality? There are two reasons for this, one having to do with the giving and the other having to do with the giver. People whose morality emerges out of a positive sense of sharing the world with others are more likely to act morally than those who experience it as a burden or a debt that must be paid. The feeling of indebtedness often leads to bitterness, and bitterness is hardly to be commended as a source of ongoing commitment to morality. I am much more likely to offer my seat to an elderly person on the bus or put extra money in my daughter's bank account for her gym registration if I am acting out of sense of solidarity or connection with them rather than out of a sense that there is a moral rule hanging over me dictating that I do so.

The other reason for focusing on the positive is that it makes *my* life, the life of the giver, go better. Not only will the beneficiary of my moral acts gain from my having a positive relation to morality; so will I. And, to be quite frank, I would much prefer my life to go better than worse. I would rather feel connected to those around me than obliged to them, and to the extent that I can weave that connection into my moral activities, I would really rather do that.

None of this means that we should never act out of a sense of debt or guilt or shame. We will all be faced with moral requirements that will be experienced as burdensome or that arise because we've done something we shouldn't have and now have to make up for it. When my offspring were younger there were times when I was obliged to attend yet another of their athletic events when I would have preferred sitting back and reading a good novel or having a drink with a friend. (Since they were all considerate enough to grow older, I now have greater access to good novels and bourbon.) I have also—haven't we all?—found myself in a position where I have had to apologize to someone I don't like because I realized I acted toward him in ways he did not deserve. Morality can be onerous or taxing at times. Nevertheless, inasmuch as we can act out of a sense of sharing with others, whether through the experience of their face or through the pleasure of common decency or through a myriad of other connections, our moral involvements will be richer for us and for those around us.

AN ETHICS OF CARE

There is a philosophical moral view that has arisen in recent years that focuses on our connection with others rather than our duties or obligations to them. It is called "care ethics" or "ethics of care." It is worth pausing over because it can assist us in coming to a better understanding of the approach we're considering here and also to some difficulties that will lead us to the considerations of the following chapter.

The ethics of care finds its roots in the writings of feminist philosophers, but its most important early expression is by the psychologist Carol Gilligan in her 1982 book *In a Different Voice*.[14] Gilligan had worked with the famous psychologist Lawrence Kohlberg, who created a theory of moral development that became the standard in psychology. His six-stage theory held that people move from self-centered motives through interpersonal connection to action grounded in principles.[15] For Kohlberg, most people did not reach the highest stages of moral development; rather they got stuck at the fourth stage, which he called "law and order." To see this, we can look at his most classic example, the Heinz dilemma, which was taken up by Gilligan to very different ends.

In the example, Heinz has a wife who is suffering from a dread disease. She needs medication that Heinz cannot afford and the druggist will not sell it to him for a lower price, even though he would still make a profit on what Heinz can offer. So Heinz breaks into the pharmacy and steals the medicine. Did Heinz do the right thing? For Kohlberg, the answer here is less important than the reasoning behind the answer. It is a question of how people think rather than simply the answer they arrive at.

Many people Kohlberg tested offered an answer that went something like this: Heinz should not steal the drug because stealing is wrong. That would put one in the "law and order" stage. To be clear here, the problem, according to people who find Heinz wrong for this reason, is not a legal one. It is not that Heinz broke the law, although that might play into people's reasoning. Rather, their reasoning is something like this: it is morally wrong to steal; Heinz stole; therefore, Heinz is morally wrong. There is a use of principles in coming to this conclusion, but the principles are without the kind of nuance that characterizes the highest two stages of moral development.

We can see reasoning like this in the current debate about undocumented immigrants. If someone responds to the issue of whether those without proper papers should be allowed to stay simply by saying, "They're illegal, so they shouldn't be here," They would be at Kohlberg's fourth stage. In this case moral and legal "law and order" would coincide.

However, when Carol Gilligan presented the Heinz dilemma to women, she noticed something unusual. Often women didn't try to answer the question but instead they resisted the terms in which the example was presented. Rather than decide the case as presented, many women asked whether there could be another approach, one that got Heinz and the druggist together in order that each could understand the situation of the other and then work out a viable solution. Gilligan notes that, "The psychology of women that has consistently been described as distinctive in its greater orientation toward relationships and interdependence implies a more contextual mode of judgment and a different moral understanding. Given the differences in women's conceptions of self and morality, women bring to the life cycle a different point of view and order human experience in terms of different priorities."[16]

This approach, according to Kohlberg's stages, might land them in stage three, the interpersonal stage. Rather than being concerned with principles, people at the interpersonal stage see themselves as obliged to those around them, those whose approval they seek to maintain and disapproval they hope to avoid. The interpersonal stage is not concerned with principles so much as the relationships in the local area in which people find themselves. However, as Gilligan saw, pigeon-holing women this way didn't really fit how they were approaching the problem. Women were not so much interested in conforming to the views of those around them as developing connections between the individuals in the situation. Rather than "rising" to the level of principle, as Kohlberg would have suggested, these women occupied a different moral space, one in which the fostering of relationships played a central moral role.

For Gilligan, this ethics of care is not an inferior form of moral development, one that must be transcended in order to achieve a morality of principles. It isn't a matter of women learning how to grow up so they can be more like men. Rather, it is an alternative but not less worthy way to take up morality. An ethics of care is not a precursor to an ethics of principles. It is another way to navigate morality, one that can stand alongside a morality of principles, sometimes as a competitor and sometimes in a complementary fashion. In developing her ethics of care, Gilligan does not claim that only women can inhabit it. Rather, she thinks that both men and women can live such an ethics. The reason that it has been characteristic of women is that women have been encouraged to focus on connection with others whereas men have been reinforced for an individualism that withdraws from connection and therefore seeks principles to undergird action.

One philosopher who articulates and ethics of care, Virginia Held, notes that we are always in relationship to one another. This is a fact that is often lost on an ethics of principles. It is as though an ethics of principles is in danger of treating each of us as an individual on their own, without relation, who then comes to others equipped with a set of moral principles which are subsequently applied to those others in our behavior (at least when we reach Kohlberg's higher stages of development). But we aren't like that. We are always already involved with many other people, navigating the world alongside and with them. According to Held, any adequate moral view needs to reflect this fact. As Held insists, "our embeddedness in familial, social, and historical contexts is basic."[17]

To see ourselves as individuals divorced from our social contexts, forming principles that are then applied to those contexts through our behavior, is, for philosophers like Held, to take things the wrong way around. This is not to say that there is no place for principles—a point to which we will return in a bit. Rather, it is to say that our morality ought to arise first and foremost out of a recognition that those our behavior affects are not only other people surrounding us but more deeply people with whom we are already in some kind of relationship or another, and moreover that those relationships already help constitute who we are.

I am a father of three kids. (Okay, they aren't kids any more, but what exactly do you call your adult offspring? Progeny? That just seems strange.) My relationship with them is not simply one of having certain obligations. It is not as though these are separate individuals that I happen to find myself surrounded by and so have to figure out what I owe to each. I am bound to my kids, caught up with them in ways that I am not caught up with other people's kids. But it's more than that. My kids help mold me into the person I am. To be a father, and more to the point to be a father to these particular kids, creates me in certain ways that being a friend to them or a father of others would not.

For instance, my oldest son is an economist. I do a lot of political organizing from the left of the political spectrum. It is easy in our day and age to become caught up in echo chambers in which we have our own views reflected back to us by our colleagues, the internet, and our particular television programs, so that we look at others who do not share our views with blank incomprehension. I myself have been seduced by this, to the point where I found unimaginable the possibility that enough people would have voted for Donald Trump to make him president. I suspect I am not alone in this. My oldest son—who did not support Trump, by the way—and I have had long conversations about economics and politics, where our views often differ. However, these conversations have made me aware of alternative ways of looking at our world, both economically and politically. They have introduced a sensitivity into my thinking about certain aspects of the world that I would not otherwise have had. This in turn has introduced certain nuances into my own thinking and acting in an important aspect of my life. Not only am I grateful for this, I am also partially constituted by it—it has taken its part in making me who I am. My other two kids have also had important effects on my life (my daughter, at once adventurous and kind; and my younger son, with more perspective than I've got), and I'm sure that readers of this book who have kids will be able to think of their own examples.

According to Held and others like her, we are constituted in good part by these relations and our moral theories ought to take this into account. How so? By offering the proper care toward the people with whom we are in relation. But immediately the question arises of how to think about such care. What is this care we are to offer those around us? Here, I think, is where an ethics of care really diverges from a more individualist morality of the kind envisioned by someone like Lawrence Kohlberg. If we are in part constituted by specific relationships, and if our moral task is to care for those with whom we are in relation, then it is impossible to say how that care should show itself outside the specificity of the relationships themselves. There is no general formula, no set of rules to guide us. We must attend to what is in front of us in its particularity.

We can think of it this way. For Kant, we must act in accordance with the categorical imperative. It does not matter who is around us, with whom we are sharing our lives. Our duties are divorced from the peculiar world we inhabit. The situation we find ourselves in may give us the raw material from which we form the categorical imperative: for instance, if I am thinking of misleading a potential buyer of my used car about how worn my brakes are, I use that to ask the question of whether such misleading could be a universal law of nature. But the character of my relationship with this person is irrelevant. It is of no concern to the Kantian whether this person is my friend, my cousin, someone who is going to use the car to rob a bank, or my uncle who is too old to be driving anyway. (Actually, this is a little oversimplified. The Kantian might argue that I can fold these things into the categorical imperative. However, the more sensitive the Kantian becomes to the specific relationship the more they begin to sound like an ethicist of care.)

For the ethics of care, it is precisely the character of the relationship that dictates how it should be attended to. This does not mean, in Held's view, that nothing general can be said about an ethics of care. She lists caring for particular others, valuing emotion rather than rejecting it, moving away from the view that the more abstract the moral reasoning the better, seeing what is often considered private as a political matter, and viewing people as relational rather than autonomous as central aspects of a framework of care.[18] But we can see that these characteristics point us toward the relationships themselves. While they hold together in forming a perspective for ethics, there is no escaping the fact that my particular relationships to others form the ground from which my sense of moral action should spring. My moral relationships to others arise from the relationships themselves.

These relationships need not be considered in terms solely of obligation. In asking how I relate to those specific others in my life, I need not always ask, "What do I owe them?" In fact, as we have seen, if I move from a more legalistic view of morality to a more positive one, I might be more inclined to ask a question like, "How might I foster this relationship?"

This keeps the relationship in view, not seeing it as something over there that requires me to act in a certain way, but instead as part of me that I have the opportunity to develop in a certain direction. Of course, there are times when obligation must take over. Who has not had to drag themselves to the grocery store because their partner is overwhelmed with a project on deadline, or had to pick up the kid once again from practice, or, just when they are settling in for the night, had a friend call for a ride from a broken-down car by the side of the road? The ethics of care allows for debt and obligation, but debt and obligation need not form the dominant framework for thinking about such ethics as it does for some traditional moral theories.

We can see this in the case of Matthew Stevenson and Derek Black. Stevenson saw an opportunity to develop a relationship, one whose direction he could not know in advance but which might offer the opportunity for something deeper than might be expected between a Jew and an anti-Semite. It wasn't that there was no relationship. The two were fellow students and knew of each other. But Stevenson offered, in a caring manner, to base the relationship on something other than the antagonism characteristic of Black's public position, an offer that was taken up by Black in his own developing ambivalence about white supremacy.

In all this, however, there is a complication that you may already have noticed. Although caring relationships and the moral tending they elicit are individual—that is, they cannot be reduced to a set of general principles—neither can they be rooted solely in the empathy one has for one's fellows. We have already seen this briefly a moment ago, when we recognized that sometimes one has to act out of duty even toward those one loves. There is more we might say about this. Sometimes acting out of care for another goes beyond empathy in the opposite direction. Not only do we sometimes have to act out of duty toward another rather than empathy; there are times we must act *against* empathy. When a parent insists that his child must brush her teeth or take a bath against all evidence of a desire to do so on the part of the child, or when a parent needs to discipline a child, this goes against the empathy one has for her. (Well, if the child complains enough, perhaps the empathy can more easily be overcome.) If a friend asks to borrow money that you know will not be paid back, making the friend guilty and straining the friendship, it may be better, if uncomfortable, to refuse the loan. Some of the most difficult moments in a love relationship can occur when one has to confront a partner on their drinking or spending habits or aggressiveness or laziness.

And there is more. There are times when one has to betray the empathy toward another for a greater social purpose. If a friend has committed a crime that goes against one's deep moral commitments, it might be better to turn the friend in rather than to care for them. When friends betray their spouses or loved ones, there are times when that betrayal should be made public, even at the cost of the friendship itself. And it can happen that in less vexed circumstances the caring a friendship or love relationship involves might be put at risk for an important social purpose.

Things can be more complicated still. One of the great social activists in Pittsburgh, where I spent ten years, is a woman you've never heard of named Molly Rush. She is a housewife who participated in the original Plowshares action, in which eight people broke into a nuclear weapons facility and banged on the warheads in a symbolic gesture reminiscent of the biblical injunction to beat one's swords into plowshares. She was a fixture on Pittsburgh's Catholic left, offering sage advice to those who wanted to involve themselves in progressive change. She always made herself available to those who needed political support or even just emotional sustenance. Both the risk of decades in prison that the Plowshares action represented and in her subsequent commitment to the progressive community, as she herself realized, diminished her ability to sustain the rich family life she would also have wanted to enjoy. And yet this sacrifice was also for her family, so that her children could enjoy a safer future.[19] For her, the commitment to a particular expression of both caring and principle clashed with another, more typical expression of caring associated with familial relationships.

So here we might ask, both within and outside the context of caring relationships, what is the relation between empathy and principle? Or, to put it in terms of current discussion, what is the balance between empathy and reason? It is a long-standing debate, one that, as we have seen, spawned the ethics of care. It has returned in contemporary discussion. Recently (at the time of writing this), the *New York Times* ran a viewpoint column on whether to trust reason or empathy in moral relationships.[20] An ethicist of care cannot avoid confronting this issue. To her credit Held does not do so. She discusses what she calls "justice" alongside care, writing, "It seems to me that justice and care as values each invoke associated clusters of moral considerations, and these considerations are different. Actual practices should usually incorporate both care and justice but with appropriately different priorities."[21] By "justice" Held means something close to the idea of a principle that conflicts with empathy. Both in and beyond caring relationships, we are sometimes called to act out of a sense of duty rather than empathy or even caring. How might we balance the two?

There are philosophical issues to be wrestled with here, and Held among others seeks to wrestle with them. That, however, is not our task. We need to ask the more pedestrian question of how to live decently among others when empathy is not enough. We have seen, in this chapter, the caring that attends to face-to-face relationships and within common decency, and we have tried to situate that caring as much as possible within a moral outlook that is grounded in positive relations with others rather than obligation and guilt. But we need to recognize that there are times when we are called to act against either our caring or at least the empathy associated with it in favor of some more pressing moral reason. Is there a way to think about how we might navigate this conflict?

USING IMAGINATION

There can be no general recipe for navigating this conflict, any more than there can be for how to go about a particular caring relationship. However, perhaps we can offer a general schema for viewing this navigation. To do so let me introduce a familiar word: imagination. We use the word imagination in many different ways. Imagining can be calling up an image. It can be thinking something is the case when it isn't. It can be positing a situation in thought that might or might not actually happen, in order to think about what it involves or what one should do. Or it can be putting oneself in the place of someone else to see what they're experiencing. As I'm using the term here, it might involve several of these uses but isn't reducible to any of them. Imagination in the sense I'm after is a reflective exercise where one is thinking about three things:

what caring would involve, what principles might be relevant, and what might be more important. It is an exercise that involves both empathy and thought, recognizing what another person (or other people) need or want and whether their needs or wants should prevail in a particular situation.

For a more traditional theorist, this kind of imagination is either unnecessary or irrelevant. It isn't that there is no type of imagination involved. The utilitarian, for instance, has to imagine possible outcomes of an act in order to weigh their relative goodness. The Kantian has to consider which aspects of a situation are the salient ones in order to form a maxim to universalize.[22] The virtue ethicist, if the situation is not an obvious one (which is the kind of situation we're considering here) is going to have to use their imagination in order to discover which virtue is the proper one to be expressed in the situation.

The imagination in play here is different. It arises in face-to-face situations where it is unclear to me how I should act, where the face of the other person or people and my relationship to them is not guide enough. It is not that their face is no guide at all—that is a key difference from traditional moral theories. Rather, it is that there seems to be more to be considered than the care that face or those faces elicit in me, and more than common decency would dictate. I bring this particular form of imagination to bear in order to help me steer through the shoals of the situation in a more morally adequate manner. In imagining things this way, I take my empathy for these others seriously, but also ask myself whether there are other principles in play that might override where my empathy would otherwise lead me.

It is possible, as we have seen, that when I consider other principles I would in certain situations act against my empathy. But it is also possible that I would not. And this is not only because my weighing would lead me back to empathy. It might also be that my weighing leads me against empathy, but that the empathy is too strong and overrides any other considerations I might bring to bear on the situation. The philosopher Susan Wolf offers a helpful example of this. "Consider," she asks of us, "the case of a woman whose son has committed a crime and who must decide whether to hide him from the police. He will suffer gravely should he be caught, but unless he is caught, another innocent man will be wrongly convicted for the crime and imprisoned."[23] There are times when we reflect, when we imagine, and yet our bonds are too strong to lead us where we think we should go.

Traditional moral theorists would object to all this, and not only the case Wolf asks us to imagine. Of course, they would reject Wolf's conclusion in that case, that the mother "had reached a point where the issue of moral approval had ceased to be decisive."[24] But even in other cases, they believe it should be the principle (or the virtue) that decides what should be done, rather than any considerations of empathy. It might be that empathy would play a role in determining the principle in the first place, but it is always the principle in the end that should predominate. Reason must decide.

In imagination as we're thinking of it here, the decisive aspect of the situation, whether empathy with the face of the other, caring as Held has conceived it, or one or another moral principle should prevail cannot be decided in advance. And this is because, in the decent life we're trying to frame in this book, principles can be guiding but need not be determinative. When we are forced into moral reflection, we consider the situation and what calls to us from it without reducing it to an exercise in intellectual moral philosophy. After all, we are part of that situation. Our empathy, our relationships, our way of being are engaged with the situation like gears in a machine. And so we reflect, consider what might be relevant, and act as best we can. It is not a matter of measuring up or not measuring up to a moral theory, but of stepping back from the immediacy of the situation, seeing what might be salient to consider, turning those saliencies over in our minds, and then acting as best we can.

If we turn from actual face-to-face encounters to virtual ones, like email, we can see the use of this kind of imagination in practice. When we email (or message, or text), we cannot see the face of the recipient. We cannot read their gestures or directly feel their humanity. And yet, traces of it are left in their words. There is clearly someone else there who has communicated with us. If we are not moved by their face, we can imagine a face there to be moved by. That imagined face can provoke our concern. This is not yet the imagination we've been discussing, but it is a step in that direction. From the imagined face there can arise a certain empathy, a caring that may have a grip, however loose, upon us.

But with email we are not in front of the person. The immediacy of our response is not necessary. We can step back and ask ourselves how to respond without being called at that moment to action. This opens the door to a reflection on principles. Of course, most of the time email doesn't require such reflection. When we're setting a time and place to meet or distributing office documents or reading about new company policies we need not worry about how to respond. But sometimes it is different. A colleague asks for assistance with a project that is not part of my job. A distant relative asks whether they can come visit for a few days. In philosophy I periodically receive email from students who are not at my university, whom I don't know, with a request to read their papers and comment on them. It is easy to blow them off; the excuses are all at hand. The distance that email—and the virtual world generally—creates offers numerous opportunities for excuse. (It also seems to offer opportunity for abuse. Think of how much easier it is to go off on somebody over email than when you're in their physical presence.)

However, if we step back from the temptations offered by distance and recognize that there is somebody on the other end of the email we've received, we can imaginatively reflect on what we ought to do, how we ought to respond. This often involves not only empathy but also principle. After all, if we acted out of empathy for every stranger, acquaintance, or distant relative that asked a favor most of us would find it difficult to get on with our lives. It might make us more nearly saintly, but this is a book about decency, not saintliness. So when we recognize that there is someone on the other end of an email we've received, we might want to reflect on what we owe and don't owe to that person. We have recourse to principle, to reason. And as we balance empathy and reason imaginatively, we'll probably find that certain requests are worth honoring and others not. That undergraduate student who read my book and sent me a short paper on it for my thoughts probably deserves a response. That relative from whom I've kept distance for good reason over all these years should probably hear that, unfortunately, I'll be out of town on the days he'll be passing through. We use imagination to orient us toward decency in these situations, situations that are not exactly face-to-face encounters but are akin to them in relevant ways.

But suppose we take a further step away from face-to-face encounters. After all, there are people with whom I have no interactions, actual or virtual. There are people who live in distant lands, people I will never meet or might never meet unless I make a particular effort. And there are people who are not yet born but who will be, and what I do has effects on how their lives go (and even, as we will see, who they are). That is to say that there are people who are distant from me in space (in fact, the overwhelming majority of them are) and others who are distant from me in time (perhaps, climate change notwithstanding, even more of them than of those in the first group). What might my moral relationship with them be? How might I act decently toward them? If I am not going to trade in my own goals, relationships, and the central projects of my life for the sake of an extreme altruism for people I have not met and might never meet, how might I orient myself morally toward them? To consider these questions is to step away from what the faces of others call me to do, from common decency toward those we share our surrounding space with, and from our virtual contacts. It opens a new set of considerations that, while not entirely divorced from what we have discussed (after all, I can call up images of the faces of those I don't know), cannot be considered in entirely the same terms.

WIDENING THE CIRCLE: MORE DISTANT OTHERS

There are billions of people on the planet and, climate change permitting, many more billions to come. I will never meet very many of them, nor will you. They will remain forever anonymous to us. At most, a few of them will appear as news items or as names in an email or on social media, perhaps with a picture attached. We will recognize them as persons, perhaps as fellows in one way or another. But we will never come face-to-face with them or even have direct contact. The framework we traced in the previous chapter has little to do with the moral relations we might have with them. We will not have the opportunity to comfort them in their sorrow, to invite them for dinner, or even to cover their cup of coffee with a napkin when they leave the room. With those distant from us in time, we will not even be on the planet when they are.

And yet we do have a moral relationship to those distant from us in space and in time. As we go about our lives, we need to take them into account. Most of us do not feel they require the same consideration as those with whom we have daily contact—although we will return to this issue shortly—

but we believe they deserve something from us, some measure of attention, however passing. They are, after all, human beings just like us—or, if they aren't yet, they will be. This seems to place some kind of claim upon us as we navigate through our own lives. It seems that we ought to take them into account as companion members of some kind of "us," even if we don't know exactly how to think of this club of ours. This is why Virginia Held insists that alongside care there is also justice to be had, justice that concerns those with whom we will not or even cannot have direct relationships.

In this chapter we reflect on our moral relationships with those distant from us in space and in time, those we will not meet and those who are not yet. We will ask what decency implies regarding our considerations of them. In thinking about these matters, it would be best to divide them into two types: those distant in space and those distant in time. Those distant in space are the people with whom we currently share the planet but whom we will not meet. They are our fellow travelers on the roads of life, but we will never cross them on the paths they trod, and perhaps never even see those paths. Nevertheless they are there among us, or we are there among them. They exist, seeking to carve out lives that our current and potential actions either affect or might affect. We can choose to ignore them in favor of caring for those around us, but most of us think that course isn't quite good enough, that it doesn't rise to the level of decency. We must ask ourselves, then, what would rise to that level? How might we be decent if not entirely altruistic to those we will never meet?

Those distant in time comprise two groups: those who have preceded us and those who will proceed us. About the former group I will have less to say. It seems to me that our moral relationship with our ancestors is more a matter of personal and often religious consideration than of moral decency. How I treat those who have preceded me, the respect that I owe them and the actions flowing from that respect, have less to do with how my behavior might affect them and more to do with the personal or religious connection I feel toward them. In an important way there is nothing I can do to affect their lives, since they are no longer living. (However, the ways I act toward them after they have died can affect their reputations, which do live on after them.) In contrast, my behavior now will have effects, perhaps very significant ones, on the lives of those who come after me.

There are those, of course, who will say that there can be disrespect, even indecency, toward the dead. I believe that such treatment is more a matter of individual belief or cultural practice than of moral decency. It may be that one feels uneasy engaging in disrespectful behavior toward a person who is no longer there or feels required to participate in certain rituals regarding the deceased, but the decency I'm interested in here is concerned with those whose lives we can affect, whether they are close to us or distant from us in space or in time.

To treat those distant from me in space and those distant from me in time as distinct can seem a bit artificial. There are actions I might perform that will have effects both on those who exist now and those who will exist later. If I participate in activities that contribute to climate change, I am likely to cause deleterious effects on those who are the victims of a warming environment now as well as those who will have to deal with a warmer climate after they are born. If I buy a large, inefficient SUV for single-person use or keep the thermostat set to high temperatures in the winter or low ones in the summer, I will contribute—in small but undeniable ways—to the misery of those who must deal with a warming planet and to those, not yet born, who will have to deal with its longer-term effects. In cases like these, the same actions will have effects both on those distant in space and on those distant in time.

Nevertheless, the distinction is worth preserving. We will consider the reason more fully and discover its implications when we discuss those distant in time. To put it simply for now, my actions may help determine who will be born, but they can't determine who is already here. If I contribute to global climate change, this will affect the behavior of those who currently exist; and in affecting their behavior, it affects who they will give birth to. So different people may arise depending on what I do, as we will see. In that way, my moral relationships with those to come are different from my relationships with those already here.

DISTANCE IN SPACE

In thinking about our moral relations with those already here, there is a small complication to note at the outset. There are many things I might do for them (and, if I form actual relationships, changing my relationship with them from distant others to face-to-face, things I might do *with* them). I want to divide these things, a bit arbitrarily perhaps, into two types. I will call the first type *benevolent*, for lack of a better word. I'm not entirely comfortable with that word, since it implies that I am going above and beyond what I might owe others morally. In thinking of myself as acting benevolently, I might consider myself to be morally superior, even altruistic in the sense described in the first chapter. But that's not how I want to use the word. Instead, let's think of benevolence as what a decent person might think necessary to do for those with whom they will likely never come into personal contact.[1] In widening the moral circle from those with whom we have direct contact, benevolence is what we would or should exhibit to others. One could think of it as a requisite form of charity, if that word weren't even worse that benevolence.

We can contrast benevolence with what can be called political involvement, which would be an intervention not for the sake of a particular individual but instead to affect the social, political, or economic structure within which a number of individuals live. In political involvement I am not reaching out to individuals directly through my behavior in a way that enhances their lives within a particular institutional arrangement; rather I am intervening on that arrangement itself. Often such intervention is collective rather than individual, although it need not be. I can protest alone or with others, lobby or campaign by myself or in a collective. And it is usually collective action that has political effects. But the distinction I want to draw is between actions I take to help others directly and those I take that will help others indirectly, through intervention into their institutional situation. Political intervention at the institutional level raises a different set of issues from those of benevolence toward individuals, and so I will leave it until we reach the fifth chapter, where we will be more prepared to discuss it. The issues raised in the previous chapter, this one, and the next will deposit us at the doorstep of political involvement.

As I have said, this distinction is a bit arbitrary. I am sure that there are readers who have immediately thought of examples of interventions that seem to partake of both benevolence and political involvement. If I donate money to an organization that is resisting political oppression, is that benevolence or politics? On the one hand, it is helpful to particular individuals who, through their struggle, are making their lives better. It seems in that way like benevolence. However, on the other hand it is money dedicated to changing the institutional structure and so seems like political involvement. Or alternatively, if I donate money to make individual lives better in a way that might be called benevolent, might their increased standard of living allow them to engage in political resistance to the oppressing structure they find themselves under—and might that in fact be my goal in donating?

For our purposes, we will designate the first example as political involvement, since the donation is directly targeted toward institutional change, and the second as benevolence, since it is directed toward individuals and only indirectly toward the creation of political resistance. However, there may well be examples that defy this distinction more doggedly. My suggestion would be to read such instances as "politically benevolent" or "benevolently political," and draw whatever conclusions might be available from both chapters.

If we turn toward benevolence, we face an immediate problem. It is a problem that we glimpsed in the first chapter, one that returns here in full force. Doesn't morality—any morality—presuppose that everyone is to be counted equally? Or, to be more precise, that everyone's *interests* are to be counted equally? Why is it more important that someone's headache should place more of a claim on my concern only because they're in an office down the hall from me rather than on another continent? To be sure, if I have a couple of aspirin lying around it might be more efficient to walk them down the hall rather than put them on a plane to someone, but that isn't a matter of morality. It's only a matter of convenience. If I were magically able to cure headaches from a distance, wouldn't I be equally obliged to treat the person on the other continent as I would the person down the hall?

And now compare the person down the hall with a headache to someone far away who is starving. And suppose that my choice is to spend money on aspirin for my colleague or on food for the person who's starving. Doesn't the greater interest of the starving person override my obligation to give the person down the hall aspirin or buy myself a cappuccino? There might be exceptions to this. I might be more obliged, as we have seen, to my family, since I have made commitments to them, implicit or explicit promises that must be kept. But aside from those, don't I owe everyone, whether near or far, the same moral consideration? Isn't everyone equally worthy of that?

This, of course, is the argument Peter Singer makes in his article "Famine, Affluence, and Morality." It is an argument that is sustained and deepened by Shelly Kagan. In his book *The Limits of Morality*, Kagan argues that there are essentially no limits to what morality can ask of us. In particular, we are to treat everyone as equally worthy of our attention, regardless of our personal relationship to them. That is, we need to act in accordance with a morality of strict impartiality. Kagan starts from the idea that all of us have at least some reason to act impartially, and so the question is whether there can be any exceptions to this, allowances to act more partially to those we care for or those closer to us in space. He considers a variety of different arguments in favor of such allowances and finds them all wanting. For example, if we argue that someone should have the option not to act in accordance with an impartial morality, that is, if one can act periodically in one's own interests, then that would seem to invite all sorts of moral abuses. But, he asks, "suppose that by murdering dear old Uncle Albert I stand to inherit one million dollars," does the cost to me of not murdering him, particularly if I really need the money, justify the murder?[2] For Kagan, such options are not defensible by themselves. They need to be nuanced in various ways, and he spends much of the rest of the book in extended arguments against any nuance that might be offered, concluding that there is no adequate defense of anything less than a strictly impartial morality.[3]

One way of confronting this view is offered by the philosopher Susan Wolf, whose work we touched on briefly in the previous chapter. In one way she agrees with Singer and Kagan: morality should be impartial, treating everyone the same way. However, in another way she departs from them. While for Singer and Kagan morality should be overriding—that is, morality should ultimately determine how we act—for Wolf this is not so. Other considerations can come into play. Violating morality, in short, is not always a bad thing. To be sure, it is always a bad thing morally. But perhaps it is not always a bad thing overall. Recall her example from the second chapter of the mother who hides her guilty child, having "reached a point where the issue of moral approval had ceased to be decisive." Wolf does not want to deny in a case like this that the woman acted immorally. Rather, she thinks we should "characterize it as a conflict *between* morality and the demands of love," adding that, "while I agree with other *im*partialists that it would be immoral for the woman to hide her son from the police, it seems to me that a willingness, in such special circumstances as these, to consider acting immorally, and even to act immorally, is compatible with the possession of a character worthy of respect and admiration."[4]

Wolf argues that alongside morality there are other values to human existence that are worth promoting, values that do not find their way into an impartial morality but which lend meaning to our existence and should be recognized as worthy to stand alongside moral values. This is an idea we saw in the first chapter.

My sympathies lie largely with Wolf on this matter,[5] but let's suppose I'm wrong. Instead, let's suppose that Singer and Kagan are correct, and so not only am I morally obliged to treat everyone equally but I am also obliged to recognize that moral considerations should be overriding in my life. In offering that aspirin instead of donating money to a hunger relief organization, I am doing the wrong thing. I should be sacrificing my own inclinations and interests—and, with a nod of the head toward care theorists—my own caring relationships in favor of the equality of everyone's interests. Suppose that is what I should do. Would I do it?

No.

I count myself as someone who is not deeply morally suspect, but I don't see myself acting in this extreme altruistic way. Now, true confession, I'm no moral saint either. I'm probably like most of the readers of this book, or perhaps most people generally. I try to do the right thing, more or less, much of the time. But I'm not going to sacrifice the entire run of my small pleasures for others who I recognize have more at stake than small pleasures. Some sacrifice, yes, but not saintly level sacrifice.

If this is true, however, then—again like most of us—I recognize that, whatever the moral claims others distant in space have on my benevolence, I am prepared to meet at least some of those claims. I should be prepared, and indeed I am prepared, to do something for people I do not know and will never meet. But if this is true, is there a way of thinking about, of framing, what I should do that can both capture what I find myself doing and guide me a little bit further in my actions?

In reflecting on this, we should probably start in a very basic place. It is a place that, given the conditions in which I am writing this, has more urgency than it might otherwise have had. However, it has never been entirely irrelevant either. This basic place is that of finding out what is going on in parts of the world distant from our own. By "distant" here I don't mean anything exotic. Rather, the idea is to discover what life is like for people outside our immediate environment. If a person lives in rural Indiana, it might do just as well to learn about life in Chicago as in Kathmandu, Dakar, or Quito. Of course, it would be great to learn about people's lives in all these places. But for the purposes of developing a moral relationship there need be only one place, a point we will return to below.

Why, though, is it more urgent now to learn about a part or parts of the world distant from our immediate environment? Those of us who live in the US, and I believe in much of the developed world, have become caught in what might be termed "niche culture," or perhaps better "niche cultures." Rather than occupying a common culture in which certain news programs, books, and movies are the more or less universal cultural currency, people now find themselves ensconced in smaller cultures of like-minded individuals. This, I should hasten to add, is not entirely a bad thing. Cultural items that would never have seen the light of day now find audiences that can engage with them. Foreign films, avant-garde novels, controversial studies of history, unclassifiable music: all these things and more are finding audiences that they would otherwise not have found because there are now outlets for them. Moreover, the existence of niche cultures make it difficult for those who control mainstream cultural outlets to stifle news or other cultural products they do not like.

There are downsides to having such niche cultures, however, and not least among them is the likelihood of people's existing views to be continually reinforced. If everyone around you agrees with you, you're less likely to reflect on your own views, confront uncomfortable facts, or engage with people who might challenge your beliefs. In such a situation, it becomes easy to start to believe things that are false, because there is no corrective. And because there is no real friction in your world, nothing challenges what you already believe. Seemingly contrary facts are easily accounted for when there is no commitment to truth—they are denied or explained by something else that is equally false.

Living in a niche culture presents an obvious challenge to living a decent life with respect to others with whom we are not in immediate contact. If we are to develop a moral relationship with them, to assist them in their lives in any way, we need to find out about those lives. That may require going outside our own bubble to learn what those lives are like.

One might argue that it would be better to learn about all kinds of lives, in that it is better to be educated about the world than not to be. Agreed. However, the issue here is not self-development but rather benevolence. Benevolence does not require general education about our entire world but rather an understanding of a part of it where our benevolence might prove helpful. However, it might be said in response that a person cannot know what would be most helpful, or perhaps even just more helpful, without knowing about more than one part of the world. Again, agreed. But the issue is not so much maximizing our benevolence as finding a way or some ways to be benevolent. Investigating the lives of others in several parts of the world might be helpful in finding that way, but it does not seem necessary to living a decent life.

Of course, someone might ask whether it is *necessary* to focus on a single part of the world as the object of one's benevolence. It isn't. Some people might *want* to learn about several other parts of the world, spreading their benevolence around. However, there are a couple of reasons to prefer narrowing the focus to one or two places. First, it offers a sense of a personal stake in the improvement of a particular group of people. There are farm workers in southern Florida—tomato pickers, to be exact—who have been struggling against profound exploitation, chemical poisoning, and even slavery for the past twenty years or so. When I learned about them, my wife and I decided to donate some money to the organization that they formed for their defense, the Coalition of Immokalee Workers.[6] Before doing that I learned more about their plight, and since the donation I have kept up with the organization's activities, even writing a column in our college newspaper supporting a national boycott they organized. I feel a deeper sense of involvement with their struggle and a more engaged sense of concern for their prevailing than I do for some other struggles for justice with which I am only passingly familiar. Although this is an example of politics rather than benevolence, I am sure that a deeper sense of involvement occurs for others who engage knowledgably in benevolent projects seeking to reduce poverty or provide educational materials or eradicate disease in other parts of the world.

A second reason for focus is related to the first. We have seen that face-to-face interaction brings with it a more vivid sense of the personhood of others, of the fact that they too have lives they are trying to lead. Learning about specific people in a specific part of the world, while it doesn't bring us face-to-face with others, at least brings us closer to them. Their lives take on a reality that might otherwise appear in too dim a light. As I found out more about the Immokalee workers, I learned names, saw pictures of people, read about their lives—both their struggles and their victories—and came to understand both individual and collective histories. This helped reinforce the idea I introduced in the first chapter: that everyone has a life to live. By focusing on a particular part of the world and those who inhabit it, that idea takes on a heightened lucidity.

The third reason for focus is in keeping with the attempt to make moral engagement, where possible, a matter of positive expression rather than guilt or mere obligation. If I have a sense of involvement with specific people in a particular place, if they become more alive for me, then whatever benevolence I express toward them is more likely to come from a feeling of solidarity with them rather than a more remote recognition or intellectual concession that I must do something to alleviate their plight. To use the term I raised in the previous chapter, I may come to *care* about those toward whom I plan to extend some benevolence. And as I come to care about them, my moral relationship with them will likely root itself more in a desire to help than in either a guilt about their plight or about how much of what I own I actually deserve or a more disinterested acknowledgment that, well, one should do something.

As before, positive moral expression will not replace all

sense of necessity or obligation. We have already seen that it does not do so for even the closest of relationships. There are times when parents just do not feel like schlepping their offspring to yet another soccer practice or school presentation or friend's birthday party. (Are there any times when they do feel like doing it?) It just has to be done. But such schlepping is not a matter purely of duty. It takes place in the context of an ongoing relationship that is meaningful for a parent, one that enlivens their life in important ways. While benevolence toward others who are distant in space will not contribute the same level of meaningfulness as someone's commitment to those with whom they share their life in a more immediate way, there is no reason to think that it cannot offer a modicum of meaningfulness that renders it less a burden and more a blessing.

So far we have focused on learning about other parts of the world where a person might offer their benevolence. We have not discussed what that benevolence might consist in. Before turning to that, however, it might be worth lingering over an objection that could be raised to the whole idea of such benevolence. Why, one might ask, offer benevolence at all to those who are distant from us in space? Why is this something that I should do unless somehow I feel like doing it in the first place? Is there some moral requirement that I extend benevolence beyond my immediate surroundings? Why not just focus on those with whom I have some immediate, that is, face-to-face, relationship?

In addressing this objection, the first thing to note is that the objection easily extends itself farther than the person raising it might like. If I ask why it might be necessary to take others who are distant from me into account, I might also ask why it is necessary to take others who are in an immediate relationship with me into account. Why offer anything to them, unless somehow I feel moved to do so? Why act morally toward those I encounter face-to-face?

There is a deeper question here, one that, in traditional philosophy, falls under the category of "Why be moral?" I will not attempt to answer that question here, assuming (an assumption of which I am skeptical) that it is even an interesting question. Instead I will assume that you recognize the importance of being morally decent to those around us. We should treat those we encounter with respect, recognizing that they have lives to live and that we ought to take that fact into account as we navigate our own way through the world. In other words, you won't have found the ideas I raised in the previous chapter to be very foreign or puzzling.

Given that recognition, the necessity of some benevolence toward others who are distant in space from us is rooted in the attempt to balance two ideas: on the one hand, others who are distant from us are just as human and have lives to live just as we do; on the other hand, we are unlikely to treat others who are distant from us with the same solicitude as those around us. The first idea is, as we have seen, a cornerstone of morality. It lies at the heart of all moral theories and is hard to imagine morality without. The second idea is one that has animated our reflections here and will continue to do so. It distinguishes what I have called decency from the extreme altruism characteristic of traditional moral theories. If we combine these two ideas we are likely to arrive at the necessity of benevolence not only toward those around us but also, to a certain extent, toward those distant from us.

There is, however, a way to flip the question around. Consider the homeless person I discussed in the previous chapter, the independent operator. Is it possible that, rather than give him money, I should take the same money and donate it to a homeless organization? Granted, I gave him only a dollar. But suppose I were to save my dollars and when I got to twenty-five or fifty of them I donated that. Wouldn't that be better? After all, I don't know whether the person I'm facing will spend the money wisely or whether the donation would help homeless people in a more efficient way. Might it not be better then to pass up the face-to-face generosity in favor of the kind of benevolence we're discussing here?

I don't think there's a ready answer to questions like these. I'm tempted to say that if we *always* pass up the homeless person we risk becoming more callous generally, but I don't have any evidence for this. However, I don't think that moral decency requires us to decide on this. If it were generally known that donating to a homeless organization was better than giving to individual homeless people (or vice versa), it would probably be best to act on that knowledge. But our goal here is simply one of decency. Giving to the homeless person and donating to a charity are likely both worth doing, and we're better off if we can feel good about doing one or the other (or a bit of both) rather than berating ourselves for our ignorance of the most efficient forms of charity.

THINKING ABOUT BENEVOLENCE

What does benevolence toward those distant from us consist in, and how far does it extend? Regarding the first question, benevolence is likely to take one (or both) of two forms: time and resources. Time involves the effort we put in to assist those who would benefit from our help. Its classic expression is in certain types of volunteer work. When someone helps make phone calls or stuff envelopes for Oxfam (does anybody stuff envelopes anymore?), when they hold fund-raising parties or do an annual CROP walk, when they bag groceries for homeless people in other neighborhoods or go door to door soliciting donations for refugee assistance, they are engaged in acts of benevolence on behalf of people they will likely never see.

None of this, of course, requires that they engage in continuous study of those on whose behalf they act. However, it is important that before committing to such efforts, a person becomes aware of what they are committing to, if for no other reason to ensure that they aren't the victim of a scam or that they agree with the particular issue they are dedicating their time to. Moreover, as we have seen, some ongoing familiarity with the issue is likely to make a person feel more connected to the people to whose benefit they are working. It will help integrate their work into their own life and will make it more likely that they will remain consistent in their own work.

Consistency is one of the hallmarks of good volunteer work. I do a lot of political organizing, an activity which we will return to in a couple of chapters but has some application here in the fact that I often tell people that consistency is the key to effectiveness. However much time a person dedicates toward their benevolence, doing it on a consistent basis—treating it like a part of their ongoing life—will result in both a more useful contribution and a greater sense that this work is part of who one is. It may, like physical exercise, start off as an effort that feels external and burdensome, but as it becomes integrated into a person's routine it becomes a source of identification rather than mere drudgery. Of course there can be drudgery involved—who, after all, looks forward to physical exercise every day of one's life?—but that drudgery is no longer a pointless grind. Instead it is part of a larger, more meaningful commitment. It is morality as expressive engagement of who a person is rather than simply an obligation or a duty.

Consistency is often more difficult when it comes to giving resources rather than time, although for people who are very busy it may be the other way around. Of course, the most common resource to offer is money, although it isn't the only one. Food drives, for instance, ask that we donate excess food rather than dollars. But money is most often, well, the currency of resource donation. People don't naturally give money on a regular basis, mostly because we often feel moved to donate when we are faced with the urgency of an issue, a natural disaster like an earthquake or tsunami or a humanitarian crisis provoked by political unrest. However, there is no reason that one cannot give money consistently to a specific cause, particularly if one retains an ongoing familiarity with that cause. In places like Palestine, Appalachia, or the indigenous areas of Canada, donating money for education or food or cultural expression can be an ongoing effort, one that is reinforced as the donator becomes familiar with the challenges faced by those who live in the regions receiving the donations. Also, many organizations are now set up for regular donations that can be taken from a bank account.

If time and money are the standard forms of benevolence toward those distant in space, how much of each should we offer? What is the proper level of benevolence or at least how can it be calculated? What is required is not so much a grid or a formula (although for those who like grids and formulas, there is nothing wrong with that) but rather a sincerity with oneself. What resources and time do I have to offer? What am I reasonably capable of? How can I integrate my efforts into my life in a way that will make them not only helpful to others but also lend meaningfulness to my own life? Where might my dedication to decency—and to others' lives—lead me? To answer these questions does not require the application of a theory but a reflection on our particular lives and the role benevolence might play in them. In this reflection, the most significant element is honesty, honesty about who we are, what we are capable of, and what draws us toward certain issues as opposed to others.

Before turning to those who are distant in time from us, let me flag an issue to which we will return in the fifth chapter. There are those who will argue that in many, perhaps most, situations where there are people in need, benevolence is not to the point. What is demanded is not benevolence but political change. The problems, it is argued, are not rooted in scarcity but rather in unjust political structures and what must be done involves political resistance rather than benevolent action. After all, unless unjust political structures are overturned, those who receive assistance will only be replaced by those who come to need it, because the situation will not have changed.

There are others who hold the opposite position. Political resistance, they say, is often utopian and ineffective. Rather than focusing on some distant future change, why not offer support or relief to those who exist here and now? Concrete change that benefits particular individuals is likely to be more effective than tilting at the windmills of many of the oppressive regimes and structures that currently exist and will likely continue to exist in the future.

I have been involved in a number of political campaigns and so am sympathetic to the first view. But I also recognize that the second view has merits. My own take, one that I don't expect necessarily to be shared, is that this debate cannot be decided on a general basis but perhaps only in particular situations. Near the end of the apartheid regime in South Africa, support for political resistance seemed very likely to be—and turned out to be—an effective route for positive involvement. In other cases, say the plight of indigenous people in northern Canada, benevolence may be the most effective form of assistance. In any event, the debate over benevolence versus resistance remains a live one. It is an issue that divides people and displays their orientation and particular hopes for the world. I cannot resolve it here; perhaps, as I said, it cannot be resolved at a general level. But it is worth recognizing, particularly for those of us who might find ourselves committed to one side or the other without reflecting seriously on the merits of those who disagree with us (perhaps because of the niche culture we occupy).

DISTANCE IN TIME

When we think of people who will exist in the future and ask about our moral relationship to them, it can feel a bit vague or disorienting. The idea of a moral relationship with those distant from us in space, as long as we widen our lens regarding the term *relationship*, is not so difficult. It isn't even that difficult to think of a moral relationship with people that we have known but who have died. Most of us, for instance, would feel ashamed to do something that desecrated the memory of a deceased grandparent or aunt. If I imagine mocking my maternal grandfather in front of friends, it makes me uneasy. Even, or perhaps especially, a parent with whom one has had an ambivalent or uncomfortable relationship can't be a source of public hilarity without uneasiness. But if we turn our attention to future people, the idea of a moral relationship gets a bit murkier.

This lack of clarity occurs for an obvious reason: future

people aren't here yet. Strictly speaking, there are no future people. There will be at least some unless the world suddenly disappears as you are reading this sentence. But now that you have read it some people who were not there before have come into existence. So there are people, but not yet future people. But if future people do not exist, how can we have some sort of moral relationship with them? How can we express ourselves morally to people who are not there?

This question, unsurprisingly, involves complications. To approach them, let's start with a second obvious fact. Just as there are no future people yet, we can also be sure that things we do now can—in fact will—have an effect on whoever shows up down the road. It might be a small effect, but our actions today do have consequences for those who will be born after we act and in fact after we die. This is true not only of those with whom we will have face-to-face relationships, but also of people we will never meet and even never hear of.

The inescapability of our effects on those anonymous people (well, anonymous to us) who will proceed us becomes clear if we reflect on one of the most important issues—some, including me, would call it *the* most important issue—of our day: human effects on the environment. That human activity has a profound effect on the environment is an undeniable fact among those who take science seriously. Also undeniably, that effect will have an impact on the lives of those who come after us. And therein lies perhaps the most important aspect of our moral relationship to those distant from us in time. While they cannot directly affect our lives (they can do so only indirectly, that is, by our taking them into account in constructing our own lives), we can affect theirs, and profoundly so. Because of this, it is not an abuse of the language to say that we have a moral relationship to them, even if that relationship is more or less one way—more a relationship *to* them rather than *with* them. After all, benevolence can also be a one-way relationship, and yet we would not be hesitant to call it a relationship for all that. What seems different about our relationship with future people from that of benevolence toward the currently living is that those future people don't exist yet. But if we hold on to the two obvious facts that there will be future people and that what we do affects how their lives will go then at least some of that sense of difference begins to dissipate.

If we attend to our effects on the environment and the impacts these might have on those who come after us, there are three effects in particular that should concern us: depletion, pollution, and climate change. We will focus on the third as perhaps the most urgent, but it is worth pausing a moment over the other two, which are in fact related to the third. Depletion occurs when we use nonrenewable environmental resources. There is, for instance, only a certain amount of fossil fuel on the planet. And there are only certain areas that have rain forests and the multiplicity of species that live in them. To the extent that we use these up or destroy them in our own living, there will be that much less left over for those who will inhabit the planet after we die. Alternatively, to the extent to which we conserve those resources we leave them to future generations to enjoy.

Depletion does not concern resources that can be replaced in one way or another. If we cut down a section of a managed forest, for instance, it can be replaced by planting new seeds of the same type. If we hunt deer, then we can foster the renewal of the deer population by setting limits on hunting seasons or creating sanctuaries where hunting is prohibited. But if we destroy large areas of a rain forest, we are likely to eliminate species of plants or animals that do not exist elsewhere and that therefore cannot be brought back into existence. This is why efforts to conserve nonrenewable resources are important. With depletion, we do not get do-overs. And so we need to be cognizant of which among our resources must be preserved because they cannot be replaced, not only for the sake of those beings who must live in those resources (an issue we will return to in the next chapter), but for the sake of those human beings who will live on the planet when we are gone.

Pollution occurs when people damage the environment by introducing harmful substances into it. Pollution is not entirely distinct from depletion—if a harmful substance destroys a limited resource, then pollution can lead to depletion—but it is not the same thing. For instance, we in the West use far too much plastic, and I understand that there are growing islands of plastic floating in our oceans, harming the aquatic life in those areas. Companies that spill chemicals into our waterways or befoul our air with their emissions are engaged in pollution. To address these issues requires not only individual moral engagement but also concerted political action, a point we will return to later. However, we know that even as individuals we can be cognizant of the waste we generate and seek to limit it. That would leave a cleaner planet for the generations that follow us and even those who are among us and still young.

My focus here though is on a different environmental issue, one that is more deeply threatening than either depletion or pollution: the challenge of what is alternately called global warming or climate change. I will use the latter term since the warming of the planet will induce a number of effects and perhaps among them a radical cooling of certain areas.

For instance, warming of the oceans could impact thermoha-
line circulation (the circulation of salt water) by adding fresh
water to the oceans. This, in turn, could lead to colder temperatures in some northern climates such as Great Britain.

We have already seen some of the effects of climate change,
from lethal drought to increasingly destructive storms. Of
course, it is difficult to ascribe any particular weather event
to climate change, since there have been numerous weather
variations over the course of history. However, I will assume
two uncontroversial truths in the discussion that follows.
First, the planet is gradually warming; second, this warming
is related to human activity. Since these truths are obvious
to all who follow the issue of climate change with any degree
of commitment (by, for example, reading the newspaper), it
seems pointless to defend them. This leaves us, though, with
the question of how to understand our individual moral roles
in climate change.

The philosopher Stephen Gardiner, in his book *The Perfect
Moral Storm* (echoing Sebastian Junger's popular book *The
Perfect Storm*, a book about the 1991 collusion of several me-
teorological events to create an enormous storm off the coast
of the US and Canada), details three converging facts about
climate change that make it so difficult to confront. The first
is that while the rich contribute the most to climate change,
they also gain from it and so have little immediate motive to
address it. Moreover, the poor, who suffer the most from it,
do not have the power to change it. The second goes directly
to the issue that concerns us here. While the beneficiaries of
climate change are in the present generation, those who will
pay the price are in future or beginning generations, and thus
many of them have not yet been born. Most of those who will
have to endure the effects of climate change are anonymous

to those who are creating it. Finally, current moral theories are unprepared to deal with climate change because they are weak on issues of intergenerational justice and how to deal with uncertainty. So in addition to lack of motive among those who benefit from climate change, there are theoretical barriers to reflecting on how to deal with it.[7]

If we are seeking decency, we should be sensitive to the effects of climate change, imagining how it might affect other people, even if those people don't exist yet. Just as we can imagine the lives of others who are distant from us in space, so we can imagine lives that will come after us, and we can empathize with those who would find themselves flooded out of their homes or dealing with severe and sustained drought or, at the limit, not having enough to eat because of a lack of arable land. This would give us at least some motivation to act to prevent further damages from climate change. But before we turn more specifically to how to think about our moral relations to those who come after us in the shadow of climate change, we should linger over a complication that shows us how deep our effects are on future generations.

The problem was first posed by the recently deceased philosopher Derek Parfit. To see it, let's start with his initial example.[8] A fourteen-year-old girl is thinking of having a child. She's advised that this would be a bad idea. After all, wouldn't a child be better off if she waited until she was older and could offer it a better life? If she has a child when she's in middle school, she will more than likely drop out of school, never get a good job, and severely limit her access to a partner that could help raise the child. It would just seem unfair to bring a child into the world under those circumstances when waiting would provide a much healthier environment.

However, against all advice, the girl goes ahead and gets

pregnant. And indeed, just as expected, the child has a difficult life. However, if you asked the child as he grew older whether he would rather not have been born, his answer would be no. For sure, his life is difficult, but nevertheless it is a life worth living. He would not have ceded it to another person.

And here's the rub. If the girl had waited to get pregnant, the child she eventually gave birth to would undoubtedly have had a better life—but it would not have been *this* child. It would have been a different one. And this child, since his life, however difficult, is worth his living, would prefer the decision that was actually made. Moreover, the child that would have been born had the girl waited is not there to complain. In fact, there is no such thing as the child that would have been born—that child does not exist anywhere. So the only person affected by the girl's decision is the child who was actually born. (Well, the other person who is affected is the girl, now mother. But it's hard to imagine a mother looking at her child and regretting that he was born.) And if that's true, then why was the decision to get pregnant the wrong one?

In this case we seem to find ourselves in an awkward, in fact ironic, moral position. It's as though the girl turned a morally inadvisable act (getting pregnant at a young age) into a morally good act simply by going ahead with it. On the one hand, it would have been better for the girl to wait. On the other hand, having not waited, it would seem, looking back on it, that it was better not to wait. After all, everyone who was affected by the girl's decision—the mother and the child—preferred that she acted in the way she did. So why should she have waited?

Having seen the dilemma in an individual case, let's widen it out to an environmental situation (as Parfit himself does, although he uses pollution rather than climate change as his example). Let's suppose that we decide not to care about our environmental impact. We drive large, gas-guzzling cars. We continue to rely on coal for a lot of our energy needs. We demand large quantities of inexpensive meat, thereby supporting the factory-scale production of animals that release high amounts of methane into the atmosphere. We fly around the country without concern for the amount of fuel that planes use. And, of course, we don't make any attempt to offset our carbon use. If we do so we will contribute to climate change. And those who come after us will have to suffer the deleterious consequences.

However, and here is the rub again, if we do that then those who come after us will be different people from those who would have come after us if we had been more attentive to the effects of climate change. Why? Because in acting differently we would have given birth to different people. A particular child, with its particular genetic makeup and prenatal environment, is the product of a particular sexual encounter at a particular time. If one doesn't get pregnant at a certain time—as the case of the girl has shown—then the child one has will be different from the child one would have had if one got pregnant then. So if we act carelessly toward the environment rather than solicitously, we will produce different offspring.

Suppose those offspring, however difficult their lives are because of our environmental negligence, nevertheless consider their lives worth living. They would rather have been born than not. After all, as difficult as life is for many people, most folks would rather have lived than not. Would we then find ourselves in the position of having justified our environmental carelessness by going ahead with it? Since the only people affected by our disregard for the environment are those who exist, and they would prefer having existed to not existing, and the only way they came into existence was through our environmental negligence, does that somehow justify our heedlessness?

Parfit has a partial answer to this problem. It requires us to think less about the particular people who exist in these different scenarios and more about the good that is generated for different people (and potential people) in them.[9] What strikes me about the puzzle, however, is not only the question of how to solve it but also what it means for us to think about how our actions affect the lives of those who will follow us. Everything we do has the potential to affect them, even to the very question of who will exist. Our actions are deeply bound to those who proceed us. We are bound to them through what we do. In this sense we are more tied to those who are distant in time than to those distant in space.

But those who are distant in space share the planet with us now; they already exist. Those who come later do not exist yet. In fact, it is odd even to say that there are "those" who do not exist yet. It is not as though there are people waiting to exist. Rather, it is that there will be people who come to life, who will come to inhabit the world, but there isn't anybody at this moment who is one of them. In this sense we are more connected to those who are distant in space than to those who are in time.

Yet our effect on those who are distant in time might be more profound. What we do can determine not only how they live but even who they are. While they cannot reciprocate our actions toward them (after all, they don't exist yet), those actions of ours are deeply related to the lives that will be lived.

Our attitudes and behavior regarding climate change

should be seen in this light. What we do will affect who is there and what being there is like for them. Those who would not be born if we act responsibly toward the environment will have no complaint; they will not be there to complain. Alternatively, those who are born if we are responsible will benefit from our current concern for the environment, and their existence will in part be the product of that concern.

And there is more. Climate change, perhaps more than any other issue, is an urgent one for those who will follow us. It has the potential to affect them catastrophically, with effects we are beginning to see now in the form of droughts, storms, rising sea levels, heat waves, and the destruction of natural habitats like the Great Barrier Reef. It is possible that in several generations the world will be far less habitable than it is now. This urgency brings with it a moral responsibility that opens up a new dimension to our reflections on how to live decently.

In thinking about decency, we have tried to avoid the rigors of extreme altruism. Rather than casting the view in terms of obligations and duties, we have sought to ask what we are called to do in our moral relationships with others, both those we circulate among and those we will never encounter. We have focused on opportunity and relationship rather than constraint and guilt. However, there are situations of urgency that may require us to return to the traditional ideas of obligation and duty. Urgency, if it is acute enough, may press us to reintroduce elements of the history of moral philosophy that thinking in terms of decency has so far allowed us to keep at least partially at bay.

To my mind, climate change has precisely that sense of urgency. It requires us to act, and to act decisively. Much of the action that would be effective is political, and we will save our political reflections for a couple of chapters. But some of it is a matter of individual morality. There are things we can do in our daily lives to mitigate the problem of climate change and therefore help ensure the well-being of those whose lives our actions will contribute to the existence of in the first place. And, to the extent that we reasonably can, we should do those things; we are obliged to; it is our duty.

Before turning to what we might do, however, it is worth asking a question that returns us to the vocabulary of traditional rigorous morality. Isn't the problem of hunger among those with whom we currently share the planet urgent? Aren't we just as morally required to address extreme poverty among those who currently exist as we are to address those who do not even exist yet? Why might we be obliged to sacrifice ourselves for those who will come after us and not do so for those who are among us now?

We can respond to this challenge in two ways. First, the enormity of the effects of climate change lend it an urgency that extreme altruism can't claim for most other issues. I should be clear here, lest I sound callous. Of course poverty and starvation are urgent, and it would be important for any of us to contribute to ending them. That is the point of benevolence. However, there is in at least one way a far greater urgency when what is at stake is the state of much of human life as we know it. Climate change threatens to wipe out entire coastal cities and to lay waste to large swaths of our current environment, making much of the earth far less inhabitable for us and forcing mass starvation and poverty along the way. If storms like Hurricane Katrina are any example, we have seen this kind of devastation already. The scale of threat from climate change is daunting; recognizing this should give us a sense of urgency that places it in a separate moral category from many other kinds of benevolence.

If I am wrong about this—or rather, if the scientific consensus is wrong about this—then, as a philosophical matter, responding to climate change would assume a status more like benevolence, and our response to it would more nearly parallel that of our moral relationships with those distant from us in space. However, I think it likely that most of the readers of this book feel as I do that the scientific consensus is worth heeding, and so conclude that there is an obligatory character to responding to it as an urgent matter.

This leads to the second response. It is in fact possible at an individual level to respond morally within the limits of decency without having to embrace extreme altruism. There is, of course, much that can be done. We can drive smaller and more efficient cars. We can make an effort to eat less meat from factory farms, which, as mentioned, generate enormous amounts of methane. (We can also, on separate grounds, refrain from buying meat from places that treat animals so egregiously. We'll return to that issue in the following chapter.) Those who can afford to do so can also seek to mitigate the effects of our carbon footprint by buying carbon offsets.

Carbon offsets are monetary contributions that a person makes to environmental causes to compensate for personal actions that result in greenhouse gas emissions. Several years ago, I became convinced that I needed to offset the greenhouse gas emissions stemming from my business air travel[10] I got online to figure out how much I needed to offset and where I could find a reputable place to buy those offsets. As a result, I now contribute to a group that works with people in Mali who build stoves that use less wood (saving forests) and emit far less smoke (reducing carbon dioxide emissions as well as reducing the risk of lung disease for those in the home).

I am not alone in this effort. An increasing number of people who recognize that they cannot or will not reduce their contributions to greenhouse gas emissions are calculating their carbon footprints and contributing in one way or another to carbon offsetting.

If I were an extreme altruist, I might refrain from flying altogether. That would be a severe strain on my job and my life. I like traveling, and the people I meet contribute to my flourishing in a significant way. But that is not all. If I were an extreme altruist, not only would I have to refrain from flying but I would *also* have to buy carbon offsets to make the world a more habitable place. As it stands, I do the latter but not the former, and so I at least come out (depending on the accuracy of my calculations) even on carbon emissions. I would rather spend the money elsewhere, but I feel obliged to do that much. For me it is a requirement of decency.

There will always be those who cannot afford to buy, and therefore should not buy, carbon offsets to match their contribution to emissions. This is where the importance of political change enters in. Although many of us contribute individually to climate change, the structure of our economy—with gas-emitting businesses, factory farming, fuel-inefficient car production, use of coal (although this is declining), and so on—makes it difficult for individuals to steer clear of contributions to climate change. If that structure does not change, individual efforts will not be enough to stem the flow of greenhouse gasses into our atmosphere. And so the onus for climate change should not be placed upon those who cannot afford to mitigate its effects. This is especially true for people who find themselves more impoverished because of their disproportionately greater exposure to the negative effects of climate change. Those who gain from climate change are usually more comfortably placed— and therefore have greater individual obligation to address it.

This leaves us with a final question before we widen the circle still further. We have discussed two issues here, benevolence toward those who are distant from us in space and obligations to those who are distant from us in time. One might ask how we should go about balancing the two. It might seem difficult to do both to a great degree, especially within the bounds of decency. If I'm paying for carbon offsets, that leaves me with less money to contribute to the eradication of malaria or river blindness or the effects of a tsunami or an earthquake or even building shelters for orphaned children in impoverished areas. And yet these are also important causes with their own urgency. How should I think about the balance between the needs of those who come after us with the needs of those who are currently with us?

I have argued that there is a seriousness and imminence to climate change that lends it a greater urgency than many other problems. However, there might be those who disagree with me, even without denying the importance of the issue. They might, for instance, find themselves gripped by the impoverishment of so many millions of people or the necessity of responding to a natural disaster, thinking that such catastrophes override the more distant effects of the warming of the planet. Or, while conceding the urgency of climate change, they may just find themselves moved by one or another current emergency and so be more likely to contribute resources to the latter than to the former.

Alternatively, certain people may be better placed to do something for people who are currently suffering than those who will suffer in the future. A doctor might be able to contribute skills or knowledge to those subject to a medical disaster, which would compete with their ability to contribute to other issues. Or an engineer might have knowledge to offer regarding a nuclear accident, like the Fukushima Daiichi nuclear disaster of 2011 caused by an earthquake followed by a tsunami. Or again, relatedly, one might live in a country where the refusal to confront climate change is so entrenched that it would be more effective to contribute one's money or skills to alleviating current miseries. (At the time of this writing, the United States may stand as a shining example of a country that steadfastly refuses to recognize the effects of climate change and its own enormous contribution to it, exemplifying Stephen Gardiner's claim that those who benefit from the warming of the planet are less likely to address it.)

For reasons of disagreement or emotional engagement or practical obstacles, then, many people may be better positioned to practice one or another form of benevolence than to address climate change. And indeed, there is certainly a need for benevolence. The urgency of climate change does not entail that *everyone* should drop all forms of benevolence to address it. Whether to adopt a practice of benevolence or seek to stem the effects of climate change will depend on factors individual to a person's history, orientation, geographical location, and resources.

However we decide to devote our time and resources, what needs to be recognized—and what most of us do recognize to one extent or another—is that beyond our face-to-face interactions with one another we are also citizens of the world. We share the planet with others we will never meet and still others who will come into existence after we pass from our own. Our moral circle extends beyond what we encounter as we go through our daily lives. This fact offers us opportunities to form bonds with others and occasionally places obligations upon us that take us outside our normal run of activities. We have moral relationships with people we will never see, indeed with people we will never be able to see.

This is not a bad thing. If we approach our lives in terms of moral decency rather than that of an onerous weight of altruism, we can see ourselves as making a contribution to the world, removing ourselves from the pettiness that often attends to quotidian living. Although for most of us Singer's endorsement of "effective altruism" is a bridge too far (or perhaps even in the wrong direction), his insight that contributing to the world can furnish us with a particular sense of meaningfulness is well taken. We need not be altruists to be citizens of the world, and our participation in this citizenry is not only beneficial to others. It might be a source of joy or meaning that cannot be had through the channels of living we find immediately around us.

So far our widening of the moral circle has taken us from those around us to those we will not meet. But all those in the circle so far have been humans. In addition to our fellow humans, however, we also share the world with other creatures, many of them sentient and even, to one degree or another, cognizant. Some of what we have discussed here—for instance, refraining from contributing to climate change through avoiding meat from factory farming where possible—would be beneficial to many of those creatures.

But the terms in which we have discussed it are in regard to human flourishing and suffering. In the next chapter we widen the moral circle in another direction, asking what decency toward nonhuman animals might consist in and how we might think and practice it.

WIDENING THE CIRCLE: NONHUMAN ANIMALS

We have a cat that lives with us. To put the matter in the traditional way, we own a cat. The idea that one should claim to "own" a living animal, and a fairly intelligent one at that, has come under some scrutiny recently, and justly so. There were humans who were once considered property, and now in most parts of the world that practice is considered barbaric. For analogous although obviously not exactly the same reasons, associating the idea of ownership with intelligent animals is receiving its fair share of scrutiny. So let me just say this: we have a cat that lives with us.

Putting it this way is not exactly right, though. It implies that the cat lives in the house with us, sharing our living quarters. But he doesn't do that. The cat, Sammy by name, lives outside our house. Well, outside and often under it. He hangs around the abandoned tree house in the backyard, sunbathes on our little deck, comes inside twice a day for breakfast and dinner before whining to return to his spacious abode outside, and generally makes himself at home in the local neighborhood.

Sammy lives outside because I am allergic to cats. Not wildly so. I can have him wandering in and out of the house at meal time without difficulties. But if he were to live inside with us then I would spend much of the day wiping my nose and eyes and perhaps scratching myself in much the same way Sammy does. So his living outside suits both of us.

You might wonder why a family with a member who is allergic to cats ever got one in the first place. I wonder the same thing. One day the rest of my family went out to a shelter and arrived home with a kitten whose name I was informed was Sammy. This was a surprise to me, since not only am I allergic to cats, I don't really like them. In fact, in general I don't like pets. I'm fine with things like fish as long as they're in small fish tanks and I don't have any responsibility for feeding them or cleaning the tank. Anything that lives outside a small contained area away from where I'm likely to sit, however, is something I would generally rather not be around. So I share any puzzlement you might have about how Sammy showed up in my house one day.

Although I do not like pets—and moreover natural environments are, to my mind, mostly to be avoided—I am mostly a vegetarian. At home I am strictly vegetarian, although when we go out I'll make the moral descent into eating fish. It took me many years to become vegetarian. I tried to do so times without number during my twenties, thirties, and forties. I think my metabolism finally slowed down enough so that I could lose the meat cravings and just retain a soft nostalgia for the taste of a cheeseburger. So I find myself to be someone who is largely a vegetarian but really doesn't like non-human animals (which should not be taken to mean that I like all human ones).

I have been asked about this. To some it seems, if not quite a contradiction, at least a bit puzzling that someone who has no real sense of connection with other animals is still committed to avoiding eating them. My more or less snarky response to this is that there are a lot of people I don't like, but I have no desire to eat any of them either. But more to the point, my reasons for vegetarianism are pretty much of the usual stock: cruelty to animals, especially in the practices of factory farming, effects on the environment, and a certain revulsion to the idea of killing a being that could have a flourishing life. I don't proselytize about vegetarianism. Nobody who has failed at being one as often as I have is in a position to do that. For me it is just a matter of trying to live decently. Even among beings I don't really like.

The question of decency regarding nonhuman animals is a vexed one. There are, to be sure, some ideals. Many more of us should probably be not only vegetarians but indeed vegans. At least as many of us as could end the practice of factory farming. With animals raised for meat in more humane circumstances the situation is more complicated. On the one hand, if we were all vegetarians such animals would never come into existence and therefore would not have had what seems to be a pleasant life for them. On the other hand, once such an animal is brought into existence, the idea of killing it for the pleasure of eating its flesh becomes more difficult to justify. But for many the idea of vegetarianism, much more veganism, while morally attractive in theory, is often hard to practice.[1] And as I mentioned a moment ago, I can relate, not only as a person who has struggled with vegetarianism but also as someone who recognizes that eating eggs and cheese from places that deal with factory farms is morally compromising by my own standards.

How then can we frame a decent if not altruistic way of

conceiving our moral relationships with nonhuman animals? If we—or at least many of us—find veganism or even vegetarianism a bridge too far, how might we conceive our relationships with and duties toward nonhuman animals in a way that does not require adherence to moral standards beyond our reach while recognizing the fact that other animals have lives to live, that they are not merely machines? Is vegetarianism the only way to fully respect other animals, or can there be different paths?

Before we grapple with these questions, we should pause a moment to recognize how much unlike machines many animals are. Recent research suggests that a lot of nonhuman animals have complex emotional and intellectual capacities, capacities that would compare favorably with some of the capacities we pride ourselves on possessing. Elephants exhibit deep grief when one of their own dies, and in fact have what seem to be funeral rituals for them. When a chimpanzee falls out of a tree it will often look around to see whether anyone else has noticed—a display of embarrassment. Birds can have extraordinary memories; some birds can remember numerous places where they have placed their food for storage. And dolphins seem to have a spoken language that some scientists are trying to decode.

MORAL INDIVIDUALISM

Given this, the most prominent position taken in philosophical discussions of our moral relations to animals asks us to take each animal, both human and nonhuman, at its own emotional and particularly intellectual level and treat it accordingly. This view has come to be called "moral individualism."[2] To see the idea, we can start by taking two different human beings. Suppose you are interacting with two people, someone of great intelligence and someone with brain damage whose intellectual level is currently that of a five-year-old. Surely you would not treat the two the same way. You wouldn't ask the brain-damaged person to do calculus or challenge them to a chess match; and you wouldn't offer to play a simple card game with the person of great intelligence. It wouldn't make sense. These are people of vastly different capabilities and in engaging with them those capabilities need to be taken into account. Our relationship, moral and otherwise, to each is distinct and is dictated by the emotional and intellectual capacities each possesses.

If, for example, we forced the person of great intelligence to exist in an environment that allowed for no intellectual stimulation beyond that of a kindergarten class, we would be doing them a moral disservice. For the brain-damaged person, placing them in such an environment might be about right, but putting them in a university classroom would only be confusing and disorienting and probably frightening for them. Moral individualism would counsel us to take our moral cues from the capacities of each individual.

But now compare the brain-damaged person with an intelligent nonhuman animal, say, a chimpanzee. On the one hand their lives are sure to have differences: things that interest chimpanzees might not be the same as things that interest the brain-damaged person. On the other hand, though, there will be a lot of overlap. They might both like playing with building blocks, for example. Neither of them can talk, although both of them can communicate. And, more to the point, the level of richness of their emotional and intellectual lives would likely be similar. They will have similar capacities, and the richness of their experience will likely be similar as well. Moreover, that richness will be at a lower level than that of the person with greater intelligence. Their emotional and intellectual lives are simpler.

If their lives are similar in this way, though, what would justify treating them differently morally? What, for instance, would justify doing painful experiments on the chimpanzee but not on the brain-damaged person (leaving aside issues like effects on the family of the brain-damaged person)? Wouldn't the chimpanzee likely suffer just as much as the person? Or, to put the point in its sharpest form, shouldn't we be willing to do to the brain-damaged person what we're willing to do to the chimpanzee?

If there is a difference here, it would be, according to moral individualism, not between the two people and the chimpanzee but instead between the person of greater intelligence and the other two. The chimpanzee and the brain-damaged person have a greater similarity of experience and of capacities than either of them have with the really intelligent person. So shouldn't the chimpanzee and the brain-damaged person be on the same moral level, and shouldn't our moral relationships with both be the same, or at least very similar?

Here our temptation is to say that there is a huge moral difference between the two. After all, the brain-damaged person and the person of great intelligence are both human and the chimpanzee is not. Doesn't that count for something morally? Doesn't the fact that the brain-damaged person is *one of us* matter for our moral relationship to them? After all, didn't we see in the previous chapter that those who are distant from us don't require the same moral treatment as those who are closer to us? And isn't being in a different species another way of being distant from us?

Moral individualists flip the issue over. As we saw in the last chapter, for thinkers like Peter Singer physical distance does not matter. We are just as obliged to someone far away from us in distance as we are to someone standing next to us. For moral individualists, then, of which Singer is also one, any analogy with physical distance may not apply because physical distance doesn't matter morally. But still, that leaves the question of whether the fact that the brain-damaged person is a fellow human being should matter for our moral relationship to them. And here the moral individualist says that it should not. Claiming the brain-damaged person to be *one of us* and so more worthy of our moral regard than the chimpanzee is what they designate with the unlovely name of *speciesism*.

If speciesism sounds like racism or sexism, it is meant to. Just as most of us find racism and sexism to be abhorrent, so the moral individualists tell us we should find speciesism to be just as abhorrent. But what is it about racism and sexism that makes them anathema to us (or those of us to whom they are anathema)? Racism and sexism call for different moral relationships toward others based on arbitrary criteria regarding who is *one of us*. For the racist, being of the same race, however defined, makes a person one of us and therefore deserving of full moral regard. For the sexist, being male makes a person one of us and therefore someone who merits full moral standing. However, as many of us have come to understand, race and sex (or gender) are arbitrary moral criteria. Those of different races and sexes or genders (as well as different sexual orientations, economic classes, physical abilities) are all *one of us* and therefore deserve our full moral regard.

This is not to say that we should treat everyone the same way. To deserve full moral regard isn't always to deserve the same treatment. There are numerous reasons that might lead me to treat people differently. If I have two aspirin and encounter two people, one of whom has a headache and the other does not, I am not really treating them with the same moral regard if I give one aspirin to each. After all, the person with the headache needs the aspirin and the other person doesn't. Similarly, if one person has mistreated another person and a second person has not, it is not a matter of full moral regard to punish both of them. Similarly, the brain-damaged person and the person of superior intelligence might be treated differently and still have the same moral regard—although, as we will see in a moment, there is a complication here.

If race and sex or gender are arbitrary criteria for saying who is one of us, however, why isn't species? Why isn't the fact of biology just as arbitrary as that of skin color or sex or gender? If a creature of another species is capable of a full and rich life, why does it deserve less regard than a brain-damaged person who is capable of more or less the same full and rich life? So, argue the moral individualists, recognizing the arbitrary character of species is an extension of the same idea that challenged racism and sexism. This does not mean, as we have just seen, that we need to treat chimpanzees just as we treat people of superior intelligence. We don't show full moral regard to a chimpanzee by allowing it to run for public office or even to vote. Instead we show it full moral regard in recognizing its capabilities and responding to those, which in this case will involve similar treatment to the brain-damaged person.

But here someone might ask whether knowing what species a creature occupies matters for understanding what those capabilities are. If I know that the animal in front of me is a chimpanzee or a dog or (okay, then) a cat, doesn't that give me some guidance as to how to treat it? Members of a particular species typically have similar abilities and needs, so shouldn't knowing their species matter for my moral approach to them?

The key word in the previous sentence is the word *typically*. Members of particular species typically or usually share certain traits and abilities which would have some bearing on our moral response to or relationship with them. However, not all members of a species are typical, and when they aren't we often find ourselves needing to respond to them differently from how we typically would. We have already seen this with the brain-damaged person, who cannot be treated as a typical adult member of our species. If a chimpanzee, for instance, happened to display particular intellectual curiosity or a dog offered more than the usual level of loyalty, we might also feel compelled to treat that chimpanzee or that dog differently. For the moral individualist, then, what is typical might be used as a rule of thumb in our moral relationships with others, but ultimately it is the character and capacities of a particular animal that should determine that relationship.

At this point, however, someone might complain about the reliance on the richness of experience that seems to substitute itself in the moral individualist's view for the idea of species. If species is an arbitrary way to determine the treatment of others or our moral relationships to them, why isn't richness of experience? Isn't that just as capricious as species membership? Why should the fact that one being has a richer experience than another be our benchmark for approaching moral relationships? In particular, and more disturbing, why should it be a guide for which beings get better treatment or worse treatment?

There is an answer to this question, one that will lead us to the most unsettling aspect of the moral individualist view. Richness of experience tells us what a being is capable of and therefore how most appropriately to respond to it. It is useless to respond to the brain-damaged person as we would to a person of superior intelligence, since the former is not capable of the richness of experience of the latter. They cannot engage in or take pleasure in many of the activities that would enhance the significance of the life of the person of greater intelligence. Relatedly, they cannot suffer some of the disappointments associated with those activities—their failure or frustration—that the latter person can. Their experience is simpler and should be treated as such. It is not that they are incapable of suffering. Both a brain-damaged person and a chimpanzee are capable of suffering. Rather, it is that they are capable of certain types of suffering and not others, whereas the person of greater intelligence, who is capable of a greater richness of experience, is also and for that reason open to greater suffering.

Here is where moral individualism begins to have bite. It not so very controversial to say that our moral relationship to other creatures should be grounded in their traits and capacities. It is more controversial to say that creatures of greater richness of experience are capable of a greater range of suffering, although that does seem to follow from the fact that they are capable of a greater range of pleasures and significances. It is more controversial still, although within the framework of moral individualism, to say that we should use greater or less capacities for suffering as a guide for who gets better and worse moral treatment. Or, to put the point in its bluntest terms, whatever we are willing to do to the chimpanzee we ought to be willing to do to the brain-damaged person but not necessarily to the person of superior intelligence, whether it be medical testing, sacrifice for a greater social goal, neglect, or whatever.

This contentious position follows from a combination of the moral individualist view and the very pedestrian idea that suffering is bad and more suffering is worse. Surely it is part of our moral relationship to others that we should seek to prevent their suffering, although we have seen some of the limits of that seeking over the past couple of chapters. If we are in a position where we must choose between two courses of action, one of which will lead to more suffering and another to less, in general we should opt for the latter. (Of course, there are plenty of exceptions.) And so suppose that we are faced with a situation where one being will suffer more than the other and yet we must sacrifice one of the two. All other things equal, we should probably sacrifice the being that will suffer less. If, for instance, our two unfortunate candidates for medical testing are the brain-damaged person and the person of greater intelligence, and if the brain-damaged person will mostly suffer from physical pain and whatever emotional pain goes along with it while the person of greater intelligence will suffer physical pain but also suffer from the loss of projects they might otherwise engage in and the anxiety about their long-term future life trajectory, there seems at least some reason to choose the brain-damaged person for experimentation (again, leaving issues of family, etc., aside).[3]

For many of us, this is difficult to accept. That the suffering of the person of superior intelligence matters more than that of a brain-damaged person runs counter to what many of us would like to think. Moreover, that we should be willing to do medical tests on such a person as readily as we would on a chimpanzee runs deeply counter to our moral instincts. Why would we want to subject a helpless person to medical testing just because they have brain damage or some other mental incapacity? All of this seems profoundly unfair.

There is a way to address this, however, from the standpoint of the moral individualist. So far, the way we have put the matter is that whatever you're willing to do to the chimpanzee you should be willing to do to the brain-damaged person. We could instead say it the other way around. Whatever you're not willing to do to the brain-damaged person you shouldn't be willing to do to the chimpanzee. And that is much closer to the view of most moral individualists. They don't commend medical experimentation on brain-damaged people but instead the ending of medical testing on chimpanzees. Peter Singer, for instance, is one of the creators of the Great Ape Project, which seeks laws to protect the life, liberty, and freedom from torture of the great apes—gorillas, chimpanzees, bonobos, and orangutans.[4]

Moral individualism, moreover, is about more than just apes and brain-damaged people and more than medical experimentation. Take the principle that we ought to prevent suffering and in situations where we have to choose we ought to choose to cause less suffering rather than more. What bearing does this have on our eating habits? If we choose to eat meat, we are contributing to immense suffering of animals, particularly animals that are raised on factory farms. (As we saw in the last chapter, we are also contributing to climate change. We will return to that issue in a different guise in a bit.) How much will we suffer if we cannot eat meat? Not much. People can learn to become vegetarians, and especially over the past half dozen years there has been a proliferation of meat substitutes that are remarkably tasty.

(Thank goodness.) On the moral individualist view, there is simply no justification for eating meat, particularly factory-farmed meat. The suffering of carnivores who do not have access to meat is in no way proportional to the suffering of the animals they eat.

Unfortunately for me, what goes for meat eating also goes for many dairy products. If I were to conform to the moral individualist view, I should really go vegan. And, although I'm not a moral individualist—although, as we will see, there is much to be gained from that perspective—I do count my dairy consumption as a moral failure.

Now if we were to be strictly philosophically minded about this, we might take issue with the principle that we ought always to cause less suffering rather than more. Here's an example. Suppose I could cause a small amount of suffering to a large number of people, say, the suffering associated with a hangnail, or instead cause a large amount of suffering to one person, say, on the order of a kidney stone. (I once had a kidney stone. I don't believe I understood what pain was before then.) Suppose further that the sum total of the hangnail sufferers was greater than the sum total of the kidney stone sufferer. Should I really cause the one person kidney stone levels of suffering? Clearly not. The principle of causing less suffering, then, does not always apply. However, in our case it's not really relevant. We're not facing situations like that, so we can go with the principle as a rule of thumb.[5]

If the moral individualist is right, then, we are obliged to become vegans and also to stop much of the medical testing we are currently engaged in. There may be forms of medical testing on certain animals that are justified by the suffering they might prevent, but far fewer of them than are currently performed. The moral individualist view would, then, lead us to a more nearly altruistic relationship with many nonhuman animals. Should we become moral individualists?

DOES DECENCY REQUIRE MORAL INDIVIDUALISM?

There are several reasons to think that we shouldn't become moral individualists, some philosophical and one practical. I don't think, though, that any of these reasons should turn us away from the core insight of moral individualism, that many animals have lives to live and that they are capable of suffering when those lives are frustrated in various ways. To see this, let's pause a moment over the criticisms.

One criticism is that in our practices we treat people differently from animals and that there are things that we might do to an animal of a different species that we would find offensive if done to a human at a much more constrained level of experience. This need not have anything to do with inflicting suffering or killing someone.[6] We would not, for instance, make someone who is brain damaged or has severe Alzheimer's eat from a bowl on the floor, even if that person would not think of this as an insult or a problem. It somehow feels undignified to treat another human this way, regardless of whether they recognize it as such. One might complain here that such treatment is against their interests, but that complaint isn't open to the moral individualist. In the case of severe brain damage or advanced Alzheimer's, as long as it would not lead to others' making them suffer it would not be against their particular interests to be treated this way. They would not be suffering from such treatment. They would not even recognize it as a humiliation. But for the rest of us it seems a humiliation of that person to make them eat from a bowl on the floor. It would be an affront to what might properly be called their "human dignity."

Or take another, starker example—that of a corpse. We do not generally treat a corpse with disrespect, even though the person that once occupied that corpse is no longer there. There is nobody to be disrespected or to suffer in the case of a corpse, but we still think it should not be treated like just any other material entity, perhaps just thrown away since it is no longer useful. If moral individualism were true, some folks argue, we could not make sense of having an obligation to treat a corpse with a certain amount of deference.

How seriously should we take these examples? Some individualists argue that, at least in the case of the corpse, treating it a particular way is a cultural hangover rather than an indication of any deep moral duty we have to the corpse. There are, for instance, other cultures that don't share the Western attitude toward corpses.[7] We might also argue that our treatment of corpses is based on the illusion that the person is somehow still there and that disrespecting the corpse is also somehow a disrespect for the person. The situation with the brain-damaged person and the person with Alzheimer's is different, and perhaps more challenging to the moral individualist. However, we might ask how challenging it really is.

Suppose that we accept that there are certain ways of treating animals that would not befit other humans, even humans who cannot recognize that ill-befittingness. As a strictly philosophical matter, this would certainly undermine moral individualism as an absolute doctrine. However, it does not do anything to undermine the core idea that other animals have lives to live and that they should not be made to suffer in those lives.[8] It seems more a nibbling around the edges of moral individualism than a full-on attack on its core view. For instance, take the case of medical testing. Moral individualists argue that we should not be willing to do to a chimpanzee what we would not be willing to do to a person of a similar level of intelligence or richness of experience. Does the idea of "human dignity" separate the person from the chimpanzee here? Can we really just import the idea of human dignity from those examples and use it to distinguish chimpanzees from brain-damaged humans when it comes to medical testing? The moral individualist would not, I think, be impressed by such an importation.

There is another objection to moral individualism, one that also doesn't undermine its core insight but is worth recognizing, in part because it's probably already occurred to many of you reading this book. I can't have the same moral relationship to all animals of the same richness of experience, because I must have some extra obligations to animals that are my technical possession. My cat, unfortunately for me, is a being with whom I have a different moral relationship from other cats. I need to feed him and, well, I need to feed him. I have no obligation to feed the other cats in the neighborhood, although at times they seem to think differently about this matter.

This different moral relationship is not just a legal one. I actually don't know what the legal requirement is regarding feeding a cat one is said to own. Maybe there's something about cruelty or neglect that has legal foundations. Nevertheless, that is not the issue. Even if there weren't such legal obligations—and my ignorance about this is evidence—I would feel as though I engaged in moral indecency if I just stopped feeding our cat. Or at least stopped feeding it when there's nobody else around to do so. Although I hate to admit this, I would feel guilty toward the cat.

The idea here is that the existence of certain relationships with animals has moral implications.[9] It can't be, then, that my moral relationship with all animals of the same richness of experience must be the same. And this is true not only of animals that I "own," but also other animals that I form relationships with. For instance, there was a feral cat that took a liking to our back porch and with it, our food, which we always left outside for Sammy. After a while, it seemed to become a resident of the outside of the house. It did not horn in on Sammy's space. It ate after Sammy was finished—Sammy made sure of that—and generally deferred to Sammy in all important matters of where to lie in the sun and when to play. At some point in all this it would have become a matter of moral neglect on our part if we just put out enough food for our cat. There would seem to be something mean-spirited in it, something morally indecent, if not profoundly so. After all, it costs us practically nothing to feed this other cat, and we had allowed it to develop a set of expectations by putting out enough food for it to eat. I would have felt wrong if I failed to put that extra bit of food in the bowl.

To be sure, this moral relationship is one that could be changed by circumstances, and in fact was. A second feral cat, one with kittens in tow, showed up on our porch a few months after the first cat. This second cat, however, was not as keen on recognizing the hierarchy necessary for communal feeding. It would chase Sammy away from the food bowl and hog the food for itself and its kittens. We could see that Sammy started losing weight. Although it is unquestionable that a diet would not have hurt our cat, this did not seem the most promising weight-loss regimen. So we had to switch our feeding practices. Now we have the feeding bowl inside the house and only Sammy can come in and eat. We can't let any other cats in, for the obvious reason that it would just repeat the problem we encountered with the outside bowl. This means we no longer feed the first feral cat, who went through a period of disappointment before wandering off to feed at the neighbors' house. But, given the new circumstances, I think our moral relationship to that cat was altered. In philosophy speak, the obligation to the feral cat was trumped by the obligation to ensure the feeding of our own cat.

Just as with human beings, then, personal relationships with other animals create moral relationships as well. And as this is true, moral individualism—the idea that the framework for how we should treat each animal solely according to its richness of experience—has its limits. (I say "the framework" here to indicate that we needn't treat all animals exactly the same way. Recall the example of the two aspirins and the person with the headache.) Moreover, these limits are not simply obligations that arise out of legal or legal-type bonds. They can arise in the course of our interaction with other animals.

Where does this leave moral individualism? As with the previous objection, I don't think it is deeply damaging to its core insight. It may be that we have different moral relationships with animals with which we have or have developed personal relationships. But that leaves intact the idea that all animals have lives to live and that if they can suffer we need to take that into account. It also leaves intact the idea that we should not cause needless suffering among animals, and that, barring special circumstances, those moral relationships are on par with the moral relationships we have with other human beings of the same richness of experience. Suppose, then, with these certain exceptions, we sought to follow moral individualism. Where would that lead us?

There are debates about the role of animals in medical testing, debates that are beyond my competence to address. Surely there would be less testing of animals if we allowed ourselves to become more aware of their experience and intelligence. Moral individualism would apply a stricter standard, though. It would appear that testing chimpanzees and some of the more intelligent animals would be out, since we wouldn't do the testing on babies and severely brain-damaged people. I suspect that there would be very little admissible testing on the standard set by moral individualism. Whether this is a good thing I will leave to the side, since I want to focus more on how it would affect our daily living.

There are two areas where moral individualism would impinge directly on our lives. First, if we were to become moral individualists, we would likely also have to become vegans, or at least restrict our meat consumption to well-treated adult animals. It's hard to square the pleasure we get out of eating meat with the misery factory-farmed animals endure and the terror many of them feel before being slaughtered in assembly-line fashion in accordance with the practice of corporate agriculture. Moreover, and to my chagrin, it is hard to square the pleasure of eating eggs and cheese, or anything made with dairy products, with the way chickens and cows are raised in corporate dairy conglomerates. Those places are equally cruel to the animals they raise and exploit.

The exception here might be meat and dairy from animals that were well-treated on farms and allowed to live a flourishing life, whatever that might be for a cow, a pig, a chicken, or whatever. The argument in favor of killing the animal, as we have seen, is that without the intention eventually to kill the animal it would never have come into existence in the first place. Therefore, it is better off to have been raised for meat than not to have come into existence. (Of course, this argument doesn't even need to be raised in the case of dairy animals. We're free and clear there.) Does the counterargument that once the animal exists it becomes morally forbidden to kill it apply in the case of well-raised animals? That is an issue that is debated among philosophers, and I will, as they say, leave that as an exercise for the reader. As a practical matter, there are very few such animals and so most of us who embrace moral individualism would likely have to become vegans.

The other area where moral individualism would impinge on us is in our treatment of the environment. In the previous chapter we saw that there are strong reasons to be protective of the environment, but these reasons concerned the sake of other human beings. Moral individualism would apply its standards to animals as well and ask us to consider whether the enjoyment we get out of an act of environmental degradation is greater than the suffering it causes among those animals who live in that environment. This is a more restrictive standard than the one from the previous chapter. Following this standard, we would have to take into account not only the environmental effects of our actions on other human beings but also their effects on other animals. It seems that those effects are widespread and deleterious. A recent scientific study reported in the *New York Times* suggests that numerous animal populations are shrinking and at risk of annihilation and that this is at least partly due to our activity, particularly with regard to climate change and shrinking habitats.[10] Moral individualism would then counsel a much more restricted range of human activity than we are currently engaged in. Among other things we would need to lower the human birth rate to something below replacement levels, severely restrict flying and driving, once again stop eating factory-farmed meat (because of the methane released on such farms), live in smaller houses, eliminate the use of plastics that contaminate the oceans, and generally be aware of the effects of our activities on a variety of natural habitats.

Moral individualism, as we can see, is a very altruistic approach to moral behavior. Here is where our practical question arises: can we—or most of us—reasonably embrace it?

Here I should—admittedly not for the first time—speak personally. As I mentioned, I tried to be a vegetarian many times in my life, and failed until I was in my mid-fifties. I tried different ways, from cold turkey to allowing myself meat once a month to visualizing what the animals I might be eating go through. Nothing seemed to work. I had meat cravings and often dreamed about meat. I think the only reason I was successful later on was that my metabolism had slowed down enough that the cravings went away. Now I have lost the taste for meat, with one exception: cheeseburgers. I still find them difficult to resist, although with a degree of resolve I have not fallen prey to temptation over the past eight or nine years. (Okay, true confession: there have been a few times when one of my offspring has left a bite or two of cheeseburger on their plate and I thought to myself, "Well, I can't help the cow now.")

And in case this sounds as though I've overcome temptation to rise to the level of my principles, I haven't. I am still not vegan, even though I know I should be. When I go out to restaurants, I allow myself to eat fish, and at home I eat dairy. And even though we try to buy free-range eggs, I understand that I should investigate what's behind that label more thoroughly and take more time to see where my cheese is coming from. And I further understand that my failing to do so probably results in cruelty to animals, cruelty that I can envision because I've studied the issue.

Moreover, I occasionally do things that I know will harm the environment for nonhuman animals. I sometimes buy plastic bottles that I don't recycle or drive my old minivan farther than I need to. And I'm not entirely sure that the carbon offsets I buy really offset all my air travel. In short, I am hardly a model for how to treat nonhuman animals.

In this I don't think I'm exceptional. Although I'm hardly the most disciplined person in the world, I am fairly good at setting and meeting goals. I don't know exactly where I fall on the range of moral self-control, but I'm probably not outside the hump of the bell curve. In that sense I'm probably representative enough, and my own anecdotal research seems to stand as a breezy type of confirmation.

If this is right, then moral individualism would be a stretch for most of us. It would be difficult for us to achieve what the moral individualists ask of us. (I have a philosopher friend who is a committed moral individualist but who, once at a restaurant, ordered the rice that had been cooked in chicken broth rather than the white rice.) And in fact I know others who are as sympathetic with many of the claims of moral individualism as I am—perhaps more so—who think of it as an ideal rather than a moral requirement. In thinking of how we might live decently, moral individualism is probably, like other moral ideals we have encountered, a bridge too far.

But then, what use might it be for us? Is it simply an ideal that we can glimpse in the distance without having the means to achieve? Should we think of it, as utilitarians and Kantians and others seek to do with their views of morality generally, as a framework for how to think about our moral relationship to nonhuman animals? And if it is to be a framework, how might we use a framework that ultimately cannot frame our behavior—or at least the behavior of most of us?

Rather than taking it as an unrealizable ideal or a framework that cannot match what it frames, we can go in another direction, taking the central insight from moral individualism and asking how best to integrate it into our daily lives. That insight, or perhaps two-fold insight, is that many nonhuman animals have lives to live and that those lives expose them to suffering.

In a very broad sense, the first part of that insight would be true of any living being. Trees have lives to live, as do amoebas. Moral individualism does not suggest that we need to take them morally into account. As we have seen in the previous chapter and this one, we might have to take them into account for the sake of other humans and nonhuman animals, but we don't have to take them into account *for their own sake*, which is what the individualism in moral individualism is all about. So the mere fact of having a life to live is not enough to elicit our moral concern.

(Let me note in passing—and I suspect I'm not the only one—that I have here and there talked with folks who ask me how I know that plants and trees don't suffer. They claim that plants often bend away from danger, for instance. I try to point out that the evidence is that suffering requires certain pain nerves that plants don't possess, but that is usually met with the response that perhaps there are other ways of suffering I don't know about. Here I find myself stumped in that way one feels stumped when you explain to someone that all the evidence in the world points to a certain conclusion and the reply is, "But how can you be sure?")

It is, then, the intersection of having a life to live with suffering that gives moral individualism its particular character, and perhaps that is an insight that we can prise apart from the doctrine and find a way to weave into our daily moral lives. Just as we can recognize that there are other people distant from us on the planet that we might take into account without becoming extreme altruists in our behavior toward them, we might also recognize that many nonhuman animals have lives to live and are capable of suffering in those lives without following the course that moral individualism commends to us.

But how might we do that? I believe the first step involves the recognition of that insight itself. This involves slightly more than what would be required in the case of people distant from us. I suspect that this recognition is more ready-to-hand than it was when I was young. With the influence of environmentalism over the past forty years and the rise of the animal rights movement, it is more difficult to avoid the recognition that animals are more than just beasts of burden or sources of taste and nourishment. This is all to the good. But what is ready to hand in our general social context should, in the formation of a morally decent relationship with nonhuman animals, become a personal recognition.

The next time you're in a grocery store you might wander over to the meat section. Take a look at each of the meats wrapped in plastic and sitting on a Styrofoam plate. Think about where it came from. That hamburger meat is part of a ground-up cow. That cow was probably fed with corn rather than the grass it would normally eat because corn is cheaper.

And because it was not eating its natural nutrition, it received injections of hormones, vitamins, and other nutrients. When it died it was probably hoisted along an assembly line where it could see its death coming and watch the deaths of the animals in front of it.

Or check out that pork loin. Pigs are intelligent animals and yet in factory-farming conditions are kept packed in together in ways that drain them both physically and emotionally. They often resort to aggressive behavior, lashing out and biting the tails of other pigs. They display every evidence of suffering throughout their lives.

One could perform the same exercise with chickens. And I probably don't need to remind you what happens to calves to produce veal. In fact, veal may be the best place to take an initial behavioral stand, to convert recognition into action. Does anyone really need to eat the flesh of a young animal that has been restricted from practically all movement during its short life to make sure its meat has that particular tenderness we associate with veal? To abjure the eating of veal is a small step, one that is perhaps not so difficult, in reminding oneself that animals really can suffer.

This is only one exercise of recognition. There are others. I am told that many indigenous groups in North America and elsewhere personalize the animals they kill for food, thanking them, often through rituals, for providing the sustenance of their meat. They are not the only ones. Religious Muslims and Jews have rituals that accompany the killing of animals, which allow them to recognize the lives of the animals that will nourish them. This is another form of acknowledgment, an appreciation of the animal and of the fact that it too has (or has had) a life. For those of us who aren't members of such groups, there need not be a ritual associated with this gratitude, although there is also no reason not to have one. That gratitude can be expressed in one's own internal monologue, something one does before buying or serving meat or even dairy.

Neither of these exercises, nor others like this, must end in people's refusing to buy or consume meat. They might well lead toward certain restrictions, asking at moments whether those chicken nuggets or that packaged ham is really necessary for the current meal. They might move one to investigate a vegetarian dish or two to be added to the family's dining repertoire. Or they might just here and there move one from the meat counter to the fish display. (In saying this I note that overfishing is a deep ecological problem. As an acquaintance of mine once said regarding food choices, it sometimes feels as though there's no port in this particular storm. As applied to fish the image seems apt.) There is no formula for decency here. There are instead insights that one might make a part of one's life and daily routine, insights that are likely to lead different people toward different behavior or routines, but point them all in the same general direction.

I have a friend who is careful in his food choices. He does not eat meat that is factory farmed. He buys free-range eggs. He tries to eat healthy food (which is more than I can claim). He also eats duck, which he very much likes. When confronted about his eating duck he explains that ducks reproduce through males raping the females. Apparently it is a violent business. Male ducks gang up on a female, sometimes starting to drown her, to make her compliant to male entry. My friend's reasoning is that in the case of ducks capital punishment in response to gang rape is a matter of just deserts. I once asked him, though, how he knew he was eating a male duck as opposed to a female duck. After all, if one kills a female duck, one that is already susceptible to rape, wouldn't that be adding death to injury? He had clearly heard this question before and had a ready response. In regard to the female duck, he said, what kind of life is that?

Would I accept this as a justification for my eating ducks, male or female? I wouldn't. But I have no particular justification for my eating fish in restaurants or dairy at home. Both my friend and I are trying to construct a decent moral relationship with nonhuman animals that we know falls short of what such a relationship ideally should be. We do, if not our best, something better than we might do.

One important consideration here is that the elimination of meat or fish from a diet can be expensive. Unfortunately, healthful eating generally costs more than unhealthful eating, at least in the US. It would be too much to ask of those among us whose budgets are strained to go very far down the nonmeat road—or, for that matter, the meat road that involves free-range animals. But even here, there are decent ways to approach meat eating. One could, for instance, avoid veal and goose-liver pate. Goose-liver pate involves a cruel force-feeding of geese. Alternatively, free-range eggs are becoming increasingly affordable, so one could buy them as an alternative—or a periodic alternative—to those from factory farms.

Turning away from our eating practices, there are other ways to show respect for the nonhuman animals among us. We have neighbors who capture feral cats and have them spayed to limit the population of unowned starving cats. Then, although they don't let them in their house, they make sure they leave food out for them. I also know some folks who volunteer at animal shelters, and others who contribute money to them. And we all know people who adopt animals from these shelters to give them better lives. Most of these people are probably not vegetarians, but they are engaged in projects of decency toward individual animals.

On another front, Temple Grandin, in addition to her discussions of her own autism, has written perceptive pieces on animal welfare, particularly during their transportation and the period where they are being led to slaughter. She claims that her own experience of being on the spectrum contributes to an understanding of animals' stress and anxiety and allows her to see ways to reduce it. Her work has been controversial among some animal rights activists who criticize her for making animal slaughter more humane rather than ending it altogether. However, for those who are not committed to vegetarianism her work provides a model for thinking about our relationships to nonhuman animals.[11]

Finally, we can look to the environment and its impact on other animals. We have already seen that addressing climate change is imperative for the sake of future generations of humans. And we are noticing that it is already having an impact, an increasingly dire one, on our current ecosystem. From droughts to heat waves to more intense hurricanes to rising sea levels, the effects of the warming of the planet are available for all to see. To the extent that we address climate change we are addressing an issue that also has effects on nonhuman animals whose environments are at risk as the planet warms. One example would be the preservation of forest land. Trees "breathe in" carbon dioxide and "breathe out" oxygen. Preserving forests, especially rain forests, both helps combat global warming and helps sustain the lives of animals who live in them.

How might this be done? People can plant trees or give money to an organization that is dedicated to conserving forest environments or one that struggles against climate change denial or one that is oriented to preserving a particular endangered species. As with our moral relationship with individual animals, there is no single road to decency. It is a matter of reflecting on the situation you find yourself in and asking what you might reasonably do to improve it.

Combining the two approaches—toward individual animals and toward the environment—opens a number of pathways to constructing different moral relationships with nonhuman animals. Some people might find it easier to maintain their focus on individual animals, trying to eat with more awareness of the effects of their diet on the animal world. Others, perhaps more politically oriented, might instead find that contributing to environmental sustainability would be more in keeping with their passions. Still others would perhaps want to draw from both approaches in forming a balance that they can live with. And, of course, there is always the question of balancing decency toward nonhuman animals with the kinds of benevolence and environmental awareness discussed in the previous chapter. (A friend of mine eats meat—he's a bit of a foodie—but then again spends much of his time seeking to make the world a better place through charitable giving and political organizing. Who am I to condemn him?) In all of this, the starting point would be a reflection on the insight offered us by moral individualism: that many nonhuman animals have lives to live and are capable of suffering when those lives are frustrated or damaged.

At the close of the previous chapter, I suggested that in a decent life we might see ourselves as citizens of the world. We might close this chapter similarly. Not only are we citizens of the world—the human world—we are also citizens of the planet. We share that planet with animals whose lives are very different from ours but nonetheless worthy of our moral concern. In living decently, it is worth our asking ourselves how that moral concern should manifest itself. There will be different answers for each of us, of course, in accordance with our personal orientations and the structures of the other projects in our lives. But if we reflect on our citizenship on the planet we might see our way to a relationship, or set of relationships, with our fellow creatures that while not altruistic at least does not give us reason to be embarrassed with ourselves.

Which brings me back to Sammy. He is getting older now and moves a bit more slowly, although when it comes to feeding time he shows surprising alacrity. I have been getting up early in recent months—perhaps as a result of my own aging—and so have often been the person who opens the door and lets him in for breakfast. When I've had to do this in the past it has been a silent ritual. I open the door, Sammy walks in and eats, I open the door, Sammy leaves. That has been the mode of our relationship for the past ten or twelve years that Sammy has been with us. (If I were more caring I would know how long he's been with us.) Over the past several months I have found myself a bit more sympathetic with him. Is it because he is getting older? Is it because after all these years I have finally come around to the fact that there is another creature living with us? Is it because we're both getting older? I really don't know. But on these early mornings when, bleary-eyed, I stumble to the kitchen door, open it, and let him in, I have found myself saying good morning to him.

I suppose it's about time.

POLITICS AND DECENCY

This is a book of morality, seeking to grapple with the question of how to be morally decent, so why include a chapter on politics? In much traditional philosophy, moral and political philosophy are treated as distinct areas. Moral philosophy discusses how we should act toward one another or how we should live, whereas political philosophy is interested in what kind of society we should live in. But, of course, these two areas are related. Political philosophy makes use of moral principles, while moral philosophy recognizes that we are all members of one or another polity.

The question I'm after here is a simple one. Because we are all members of polities, because we all inhabit what is more or less accurately called a public space—or several public spaces—we need to ask what it is to act decently within them. We have considered ways of acting decently toward individual others, both near and distant, both human and nonhuman. But each of us is also a member of a number of larger collectives—local, national, and international. What might decency involve within these memberships? How might we engage in our common spaces in ways that might roughly be called proper; that is, neither neglecting them nor making them the center of our existence?

We cannot ask this question in the abstract. That is to say, we cannot abstract from our current political situation in order to ask what political decency in some very general way might involve. In the previous chapters we were able to say some more or less general things about moral decency, about how to exhibit common decency, how to take account of others who live far away, or how to relate to nonhuman animals. Of course, all these things are, to an extent, contextual as well. Common decency, as we saw, runs along distinct pathways in different cultures. The fact of climate change imposes certain moral tasks on us regarding future generations and nonhuman animals that its absence would not. If there were no poverty in other parts of the world then our moral relationship to those distant from us would change. In no part of our moral life, then, can we abstract completely away from particular circumstances in order to ask how to be morally decent.

However, when it comes to politics we need to remain even closer to the ground. Politics concerns the structure of our common situation—its economic structure, its race and gender relationships, its form of governance, the ethos of political discourse, and so on. We cannot ask how to act decently without taking the structure of our situation into account.

There is a further problem here, one that you have probably already recognized in the previous paragraph. There is no such thing as "our common situation." Different countries, and even different social groupings within those societies, have different political situations. In the United States, for instance, we cannot think about our political situation without taking into account the history of racial oppression. To attempt to ask the question of acting in a politically decent manner without reflecting on race would be to miss a central defining aspect of that situation. That would not be true, for instance, in the Philippines or in Sweden. Those countries have their own histories with their own difficulties, but there is no role for race equivalent to the one it plays in the US.

This raises the challenge of how to approach a reflection on political decency, since the lessons we might draw from thinking about one situation will likely have limited relevance for other situations. This challenge is a real one, but I believe we can meet it more or less successfully. While I will focus mostly on the current political situation in the United States, there are two ways in which what I say here might find resonance for those inhabiting other political spaces. First, some of the central concepts we will make use of here— civility and nonviolence, especially—can be applied in many different contexts, although those applications will have their own nuances.

Second, there are some problems that are similar or have equivalents in other countries. Although Denmark, for instance, does not have a history of racial difficulties—until recently it was a homogeneous society—it is now in the midst of dealing with an immigrant population that does not share its particular cultural assumptions. A reflection on US race relations can offer insights for Danish attempts to develop or maintain political decency regarding its newer population. Those insights won't be direct; they will have to be filtered through the specific Danish context. But their relevance is readily apparent.

One caveat, though, before we delve in. Political situations will often look different depending on the perspective from which they are seen. I am a white male from a fairly privileged background and, although I have spent a good bit of time organizing alongside African Americans, Palestinians, LGBTQ folks, and others, I cannot help seeing things from a certain vantage point. In fact, it is *because* I have spent that time organizing that I have learned this. This is not to say that I cannot learn anything about the experience of others. Of course I can. We all can. However, in what follows there will necessarily emerge a certain perspective, one that might look different if it were written by, say, an African American woman.

OUR CURRENT POLITICAL CONTEXT

So where are we now? I am writing these lines in the summer of 2017. Our president is Donald Trump. One characteristic many have associated with him—and I am sympathetic with this—is his indecency toward others: women, African Americans, Muslims, and just about anyone who disagrees with him. It would be easy to lay all political indecency at his doorstep, but it would be a mistake. Indecency is part of our larger political context, one that cries out for our understanding.

This context, at least in its broad outlines, is not difficult to grasp. We should recall that the previous president, Barack Obama, was often the object of barely concealed racism, not the least from Donald Trump himself. Moreover, the Republicans who opposed him in office declared at the outset of his presidency that their goal was that he should fail. There was no attempt to work with him, to compromise, or to seek common ground. There was among many in Congress a willingness to shut down the government in order to oppose him. The orientation of almost the entirety of the Republican party and its supporters was one analogous to war, where there are two sides and no common ground in a game that is zero sum. There is no possibility of everyone winning. If they win, we lose, and vice versa. If politics is defined as the art of compromise, then it has been a while since we've seen any politics here in the US.

In a situation like this, many of the normative constraints on behavior come loose. Things that were not acceptable to say or to do under other circumstances become permissible. It is not that there are no normative constraints on behavior. Murdering one's political opponent is still forbidden. However, the space of admissible speech and behavior becomes significantly wider. It comes to include things that I have called here indecent.

This indecency does not confine itself to the sphere of traditional politics. It is expressed, for instance, in the open and even casual racism that has re-emerged in recent years: verbal slurs against Muslims and African Americans, racist slogans painted on people's doors or cars or in public places, claims that those who continue to be marginalized are in fact privileged in our society.

So far I have discussed the emergence of indecency as though it were solely a phenomenon of the political right. And I will admit here that my politics tilts toward the left. But the left has not been without blame in contributing to indecency. This can be seen most spectacularly in a couple of violent attempts to prevent right-wing speakers from addressing college audiences. At the University of California–Berkeley, for instance, violent demonstrations forced the cancellation of scheduled speaker Milo Yiannopoulos, an admittedly odious personage who was recently found to endorse sex with boys as young as thirteen years old.[1] This demonstration, which was nationally televised, did nothing to endear the

left to the US populace, but it did give Yiannopoulos the kind
of television coverage and public exposure he clearly cov-
eted. (By contrast, when Yiannopoulos spoke at my university, Clemson, progressive organizers on campus decided not
to protest his speech. Many people who live in and around
Clemson—and much of the rest of the nation—never knew
he had been here.)

This incident was followed by another one at Middlebury
College, where a protest shut down a speech by conservative
Charles Murray and in which a professor was injured.[2] In
the wake of these events, there has been a vigorous debate
about what constitutes "free speech" and whether the invited
speakers were or were not entitled to express opinions that
many find to be contrary to informed public debate. However,
I would like to remain focused on the issue of decency. Protests such as these contribute to the incivility that has come
to characterize US political culture, and, often to a lesser extent, political culture in a number of European countries.

I am not saying that the left and right are equally culpable
in the creation of such a culture. It seems obvious to me
that the indecency characterizing our political space is far
more a product of a right-wing movement marked by racism,
xenophobia, anti-LGBTQ sentiment, and misogyny than a
left which has rarely been more than marginal in the US.
However, the response to this indecency has sometimes contained its own elements of incivility, elements that to my
mind are neither tactically wise nor—the relevant point for
us—morally decent.

APPROACHING POLITICAL DECENCY

How might we begin to frame a decent politics, or more precisely for our purposes a decent way of behaving politically?

As a first step let us return to the underlying theme proposed in chapter 1: moral action recognizes that there are others in the world who have lives to live. We share the world—the narrow world within which we conduct our daily lives, the wider world that forms our political culture, and the planet— with others who, like us, are trying to construct lives that are worth their living. As I put it in the first chapter, people seek "to engage in projects and relationships that unfold over time; to be aware of one's death in a way that affects how one sees the arc of one's life; to have biological needs like food, shelter, and sleep; to have basic psychological needs like care and a sense of attachment to one's surroundings."[3] In previous chapters we have asked how to integrate that fact into our own living such that even though we do not necessarily become altruists we are nevertheless sensitive to the fact of sharing our world with others who are like us in this way.

When it comes to politics there is an added dimension that complicates matters. Some of these others with whom we share the world do not see it in the same way we do. Further, this difference in vision can affect the space in which we live. There are many different manners of seeing the world in divergent ways. One can consider ice cream an excellent dessert while another would argue instead for cake. Some consider literature to be better than psychology for understanding people, while others would demur. It is entirely possible (although history has not been kind in this regard) for people to differ in their religious views and yet still engage with one another in ways that are comfortable for everyone. But when it comes to politics the situation is often different. People of different political views can coexist peacefully, even comfortably. The difficulty begins when these political views are not simply different but also conflicting.

Politics involves what we might call the normative construction of shared space. That is, in politics we are concerned with what the common space we occupy should look like. What I am calling "shared" or "common" space, I should add, is not the same thing as what is often called "public space" as opposed to "private space." As many feminist thinkers have pointed out, what is often considered private space, for example the home, has political dimensions that are continuous with public space. Our shared or common space, then, is all of our space inasmuch as it is shared.

Once we recognize that politics concerns this entire shared space and that we often disagree with one another about what this shared space should look like, we can see that the stakes of politics are both numerous and often prodigious. They concern questions as diverse as whether we should tax the wealthy at a higher rate than the poor, whether abortion should be permitted, how to engage with humanitarian crises abroad, and what the proper criteria are for citizenship. Disagreements about these matters are disagreements about the proper character of the social field we occupy with one another, about how we should live with one another. In contrast to, say, common decency, there is an element of our political interactions that can be threatening. It is no wonder that people often avoid political discussion or that it can descend so quickly into vitriol.

The problem we are confronting—or failing to confront—here in the US is that vitriol has become the very ethos of our political behavior. Our political relationships are conducted not so much through disagreement as through anger and the related desire to silence all opposition. And so we find ourselves currently in a common space that seems irreconcilably fractured, a sort of war of some against some.

To participate in or contribute to this ethos, even though the stakes for each of us is high, is to be politically indecent. It is to refuse to recognize that others also occupy this space and are trying to conduct their lives in it, much less that they have their own viewpoints that are often legitimate at least in their own eyes. And so we might say that the first task of political decency—although, as we shall see, not the last—is civility.

How might we characterize political civility?[4] At its most basic level, it will involve behavior that stems from a recognition that other people with whom I inhabit a common space have lives to live, just as I do. This, of course, is the guiding thread of our various reflections here, and so doesn't need further elaboration. In light of the problem of normative disagreement, though, we need immediately to add something to this, something that will speak to such disagreement. What we might add is that the fact that there are those among these other people who disagree with me on political matters does not diminish the legitimacy of their viewpoints. They may be mistaken or even cynical in their views, but the sole fact that we disagree is not enough to dismiss them. Disagreement itself is not enough to prompt confrontation. There are—and we shall return to this—disagreements in which one side is indeed egregiously wrong or untrustworthy or oppressive, and there must be ways of confronting those who act this way. However, this needs to be distinguished from the mere fact that there is disagreement.

If we make this distinction then we can make our way to a second step in political civility. In addition to recognizing the other as having a life to live in a common space, we can, at least as a default, take disagreement to be precisely that: disagreement. When I have a disagreement with people I know,

I have several ways I might navigate that disagreement. If nothing much is at stake, then I can ignore it or accommodate it. When my friend leaves a smaller tip at a restaurant than I would have desired or turns the heat up a little too high while we're driving or vents to me about someone I don't know well in a way that feels a bit too disparaging, I can let these things go. However, as we have seen, politics often does not concern matters with smaller stakes—although sometimes smaller stakes can be mistaken for larger ones. So what do I do when a friend and I disagree about something important? I talk to them, but in a way that shows that while we may disagree I recognize them as having a viewpoint that is worth recognizing even if I consider it mistaken. I show them, often through my demeanor rather than my words, that I do not take them to be dumb or deceitful but rather, to my mind, simply mistaken. (Of course, none of us do this without fail, but we almost always regret it when we don't.) In short, I take my friend seriously as another person.

Part of taking them seriously as another person is to be open to the possibility that it is *I* who might be mistaken. This is a complicated attitude, so we should linger over it a moment. To say that I am open to the possibility of being mistaken does not mean that I don't really believe what I believe. I really do believe, for example, that there should be a progressive tax structure and that affirmative action fosters a healthy diversity and that if we institute free public health care it won't create incentives for too many people to abuse the medical system. But I believe these things in a way that scientists believe what they believe: they stand as true for me until I am convinced otherwise. New evidence may perhaps challenge my beliefs in ways that I cannot foresee—after all, if I could foresee them I would change my beliefs now. The difference between a conversation with a political opponent and a scientist is that in the latter case it is new scientific evidence that can shake a belief whereas in the former case it is a good argument.

In short, my relation to my own beliefs, whether normative or factual, is one of fallibility. My beliefs may be true—I certainly take them to be true. But they are also fallible, open to revision by my further experience. If I approach those with whom I disagree with this attitude, I am more likely to be civil toward them rather than patronizingly trying to explain to them why they're wrong or dismissing them as just stupid or benighted.

In a polarized political atmosphere such as ours, it is difficult to maintain such an attitude. We are all encouraged to move to our political corner and fight from there, taking on all comers and ceding no ground. But in fact it is precisely at moments like this when the attitude of civility is most necessary. We in the US are often said currently to live in two overlapping countries, a red conservative one and a blue liberal one. These two countries may overlap geographically (although there is some separation, for example between country red an urban blue), but not socially. And indeed since the election of Donald Trump as president it is increasingly difficult to open up political conversations with those with whom we might disagree. Nevertheless, if we are to be able to inhabit a common space with one another it is imperative that we develop an attitude of civility, taking others with whom we disagree seriously as people who have their own lives to live and who may have cottoned on to some bit of truth that we have missed.

Because this attitude of civility can be difficult to display, particularly in circumstances of political polarization, there should be places of respite for it as well. I am not suggesting that we always feel fallible in our beliefs, that at every moment we assume the mantle of civility in our thought about others. At home with our partners or among like-minded friends we often need to blow off steam, agreeing that this or that public figure is an idiot or just plain evil. (At the limit, I suppose that it is even possible to display civility outwardly while thinking to oneself that the person one is talking to is an idiot or evil, but that is a tougher trick to pull off successfully.) Without these outlets, civility could become a more altruistic demand on us. However, in order to be politically civil toward others, we need to habituate our behavior enough so that it becomes something we're capable of in our common space. Civil disagreement with another person in a political atmosphere of shouting and recrimination, and indeed violence, is not a demeanor that we can just pick up without practice or thought. We need to instill in ourselves practices of civility to be able to display them in the common space we share with others who are often very different from us.

However, there are limits to this type of civility. While there may not be limits to the underlying attitude of civility—that others with whom I disagree have lives to live and that they may have a grip on some corner of the truth that I have missed—there are certainly limits to what can be discussed within a framework of civility. For my part, and I believe I am not alone in this, views that are racist or homophobic or misogynistic or that blame the poor for their poverty or celebrate winning at all costs are not up for discussion. And these are all attitudes—and in fact policies—that are current in the US political context. These are not, to my mind, matters of conversation in which I take the attitude that I could be wrong. I do not say to myself, maybe I'm mistaken in my view that African Americans as a group are equally intelligent to people of European descent or in my view that people in poverty do not deserve their lot. But how then is it possible to take this attitude and remain civil? How can I be politically committed to act on a position I refuse to question while remaining politically decent? How do I recognize another person who is racist or homophobic as someone who has a life to live while at the same time challenging not simply their beliefs (or perhaps not their beliefs at all) but their actions?

Before addressing this question, we should pause to recognize two important aspects of phenomena like racism, sexism, homophobia, and callousness toward poverty. These are all ways of denying the full humanity of others. Take the most obvious instance, racism. At the extreme—slavery—there is a denial that the enslaved person is really a person at all, or at least a person in the same way the enslaver is. Of course in most parts of the world we no longer face the problem of traditional slavery.[5] However, when white people think of those of African descent as lazy or less intelligent or when they do not want African Americans living near them or when, as is often documented, African Americans are turned away from job opportunities at a greater rate than less qualified whites,[6] it is clear that many white people do not see African Americans as having a life to live in the same way that they do. There is a refusal to recognize African Americans as seeking to create a flourishing or meaningful life for themselves in the same way that whites do.

What holds for racism holds as well, although in different ways, for sexism, homophobia, what has come to be called "ableism," and indifference or hostility toward the poor. The often pervasive attitude that women are not as intelligent or committed to work as men, the refusal to recognize gay marriage as equally worthy as traditional male/female marriage, the assumption that someone with a physical disability is less intelligent or emotionally nuanced as those without a disability, or the attitude that poor people are impoverished because they don't care to better themselves: these are all expressions of a mindset that perceives others as less fully human than oneself.

This is not all. There is a second aspect of these attitudes that we should recognize, an aspect that gives them their particularly political character—that is, their character as part of the ethos of our common space. Individuals don't just happen to be racist or homophobic and so on. They are not born that way. These attitudes are developed in a cultural space that encourages them and that weaves the oppression of marginalized groups into the very fabric of a society. It is sometimes said, for instance, that when police in the US kill innocent African Americans, it is because of a few "bad apples" in the police force. However, the use of police to suppress African Americans has a very long history in my country, a history whose effects have bearing on every person who puts on a police uniform. For a person in the police not to be racist (and this includes, in my admittedly anecdotal experience, African American police officers) requires a conscious effort to resist those effects.

While recent police actions are a vivid demonstration that our society is characterized by racism, it can be seen underlying other racist attitudes as well, and further in the attitudes that underlie sexism, homophobia, ableism, and insensitivity toward poverty. Moreover, it can be seen not just in the attitudes of individual people but in the very structure of the society itself. For instance, over the past decades the US has seen a massive transfer of wealth to those who are already wealthy, and away from everyone else.[7] This has left stagnation for the poor in its wake, a stagnation that at the moment of this writing is still not being addressed and in fact may worsen if certain policies are enacted. This stagnation itself in the midst of plenty is a social refusal to recognize the full humanity of those who are impoverished, a refusal that is not a matter of individual attitude but of the social structure itself. To be sure, such a refusal often informs and interacts with individual attitudes, but it would be a failure of perception if we did not observe that practices that refuse to recognize the full humanity of others are not just a matter of individual attitudes but instead reflect something deeper and more pervasive in our society.

So the question we want to confront becomes a little more nuanced. Rather than asking how to confront racism and so on while still recognizing that the racist has a life to live, we must ask how to confront these attitudes and practices while not mirroring them in our own behavior. How do we step beyond mere civility in addressing the dehumanization of those who exist in our common space without violating the fundamental orientation that civility embraces?

THE ROLE OF NONVIOLENCE

Fortunately for us, we do not need to craft this way of confronting dehumanization, since it already exists. It goes under the broad name of *nonviolence*, and it has a long and deep history. It is a history rooted in struggles of those who are marginalized or disenfranchised. The two most famous nonviolent movements of resistance—the Indian Independence Movement and the US Civil Rights Movement—arose among people who were oppressed, often by forces of extreme violence (the British army and American Southern racists). This legacy continued with the protests that brought down Ferdinand Marcos in the Philippines, challenged President Hosni Mubarak in Egypt, sustained Occupy in New York and other cities, and appears in the present day with many of the activities of groups like Black Lives Matter. We don't need to investigate the rich history of nonviolence,[8] but getting a sense of what nonviolence is and can be will point us toward ways of resisting practices and structures that push people toward the margins without becoming like the people or structures we are resisting. This is not to say that nonviolence is the only acceptable means of political action; we need not be pacifists. But in seeking to understand political decency, it will play the central role.

It might be worth beginning a discussion of nonviolence by saying a little bit about what nonviolence is not. For starters, nonviolence is not remaining quiescent or docile in the face of power. Mohandas Gandhi, one of the two great twentieth-century theorists and practitioners of nonviolence (the other being Martin Luther King Jr.), explicitly rejected the term "passive resistance" as a synonym for nonviolence.[9] Nonviolence is active and often very creative. It seeks to resist oppression, whether individual or institutional, through means that do not involve the violence often associated with such oppression. This requires real activity, not passivity.

The other view of nonviolence that we should be wary of is a more romantic one, that nonviolence is necessarily a matter of standing up courageously against the blows of an evil enemy and attracting the attention and admiration of the world. It is not that there is no truth to this romantic view. Many of the iconic images and stories associated with nonviolence are romantic ones, from Gandhi's Salt March to the Freedom Riders and the lunch counter sit-ins of the US Civil

Rights Movement. And indeed these are inspiring examples of nonviolence. However, if we think of nonviolence solely in these terms then we're relegating it to the moral realm of altruism. People who engaged in the Salt March, the Freedom Rides, the lunch counter sit-ins and many other campaigns of nonviolence during the Indian Independence and US Civil Rights Movements were beaten and publicly reviled. They were often trained beforehand in methods of nonviolent resistance in order to be able to withstand abuse while remaining steadfast and yet not retaliating. If this were all there was to nonviolence, it would lead us well beyond decency into more morally elevated territory.

While the type of noncooperation characteristic of the romantic views people have of nonviolence are certainly inspiring, nonviolence can involve more pedestrian activities. Public demonstrations are often expressions of nonviolence. Boycotting a company that engages in egregious practices like environmental degradation or callous treatment of its employees is a form of nonviolence. Campaigns of letter-writing on behalf of political prisoners of the kind Amnesty International organizes are examples of nonviolence. Reaching out to organizations that work in marginalized communities is an active way to engage in nonviolence. As I write these lines, there are two groups in an African American community in a nearby city that are trying to get streetlamps along a section of road in a poor area where many people have been killed at night by cars whose drivers cannot see them. I have met with organizers from these groups and have let others, particularly middle-class white folks, know about their campaign. Many of them are interested in assisting and have asked what they can do. Putting oneself at the disposal of groups like these is a way of engaging in nonviolent politics that offers solidarity with those who are struggling for justice on a scale that is smaller than the American Civil Rights Movement but nevertheless makes an important difference in people's lives.

At the outset, one usually attempts to persuade those who are preserving an oppressive social arrangement to stop doing so. These attempts are also acts of nonviolence. In fact, both Gandhi and King insisted that before undertaking a campaign of noncooperation it is incumbent on people to seek to persuade their adversaries of the moral mistake those adversaries are making. For Gandhi, the necessity of persuasion was rooted in the idea we discussed above that one cannot assume one has access to the whole truth. In attempting to persuade an adversary one might discover that there is more to the adversary's position than one had previously thought, or at least that the adversary, while mistaken, has a more sincere commitment to their position than it might have otherwise seemed. At this point we are assuming that civil persuasion has failed and further measures are needed. However, the insight behind Gandhi's position—that nobody has access to the full truth—can continue to inform our actions.

In what follows I will stretch the concept of nonviolence a bit to encompass some of the activities we discussed in previous chapters, but I will try to preserve its core idea, one that has animated our discussions throughout: that others have lives to live and that acting decently involves a sensitivity to that fact. In my own view, that sensitivity as it is expressed in nonviolent action involves respecting both the dignity and the equality of others.[10] Let us look at each in turn.

Dignity, as we might understand it here, has two sides. One side involves the treatment of others, and the other involves one's own behavior. There is treating another as though they possess the quality of dignity and there is acting in a dignified manner. Although these are related, they are not the same thing.

Treating another as though they possess dignity is grounded in the philosophical idea of an intrinsic value. An intrinsic value can be contrasted with an instrumental value. Money, for instance, has only an instrumental value—it has value only inasmuch as it can obtain something else that is valuable. It has no value on its own. If we destroyed a piece of money, say by throwing away a penny, we don't do it any harm. We haven't violated it somehow. What has only instrumental value doesn't require us to treat it in any particular way, except perhaps inasmuch as it would be helpful as a means to another end. We might put this by saying that anything that has only instrumental value has no value *in itself.*

Intrinsic value, by contrast, is a value something has in itself, a value that is to be respected not simply because of what else it can get us. Some people think that fine art has an intrinsic value. Van Gogh's *Starry Night*, they would say, has the intrinsic value of beauty. Its value goes beyond the pleasure it gives anyone—that is only instrumental value. Rather, these people argue, even if there were nobody to see it, it would still be wrong to destroy the painting. *Starry Night* would still possess value in itself. One might say in a philosophical vein that a world in which *Starry Night* exists is a better world than one in which it didn't, even if there were no human beings in either world to appreciate its existence.

Whether or not folks agree that art has intrinsic value, almost everyone agrees that human beings do. What that value is can be a matter of dispute. Immanuel Kant thought that the intrinsic value human beings possessed, the value that must be respected, is rationality. In fact, he thought that any being that possessed rationality would have the same intrinsic value as human beings, and so didn't necessarily restrict this type of intrinsic value to humans. For Kant, to have dignity was to have rationality. Other philosophers have found the idea of rationality too restrictive to stand as the intrinsic value of human beings. After all, many small children and—to return to our example from last chapter—people with brain damage do not have much in the way of rationality. Does that mean that we can treat them as less than fully human, or that they do not possess the intrinsic value of other human beings?

We saw in the previous chapter that moral individualists might believe that small children and people with severe brain damage do not possess the richness of experience of others (richness of experience roughly being their candidate for intrinsic value). However, for them the goal was not to eliminate these humans from moral consideration but instead to raise other beings up for *greater* moral consideration. If we choose rationality as the intrinsic value possessed by human beings, that path isn't open to us. Humans that were less than fully rational would simply not be human in the sense required to possess intrinsic value.

So what should stand as the intrinsic value possessed by human beings? My proposal is one that we have already seen, in this chapter and previous ones: the capacity "to engage in projects and relationships that unfold over time; to be aware of one's death in a way that affects how one sees the arc of one's life; to have biological needs like food, shelter, and sleep; to have basic psychological needs like care and a sense of attachment to one's surroundings." This is a less restrictive criterion than rationality, or at least less than the kind of full-blooded rationality that philosophers like Kant have in mind. However, it does, I hope, capture what many of us feel is the intrinsic value to be respected in human beings. It is what gives human beings dignity. To treat a human being as having dignity, then, is to treat them as possessing the intrinsic value of the capacity to engage in projects and so on.

What does this mean for how we should treat our fellow human beings? Although we will be able to offer a more specific answer to this question in a bit, after our discussion of equality, we might briefly characterize this by saying that there are certain limits beyond which our treatment of human beings cannot go, unless there are extraordinary circumstances. (Self-defense against an attack by another human being might be such a circumstance.) To treat people with dignity requires that we not shut people off from developing important life projects and significant relationships or bar them from meeting their basic biological needs. In order to thrive people must, in addition to fulfilling needs like food, sleep, and shelter, be able to engage in projects of various sorts that unfold over time, often with other people who matter to them. These projects can be of various kinds: friendships, meaningful work, love relationships, even hobbies. To prevent people from doing these things is to fail to acknowledge their dignity, that is their intrinsic value as human beings.

It is important to recognize, however, that respecting the dignity of another does not require that we are never coercive toward them. This is an important insight, one that some of Gandhi's followers themselves failed to recognize.[11] Projects that are important to people may include the oppression of others or at least participating in projects among whose effects, whether they know it or not, is the oppression of others. Preserving the dignity of another does not mean that we must allow them to do that. Through nonviolent means we can seek to prevent their engaging in these projects, but we must not prevent their having access to other projects, projects that don't oppress others. We might, for instance, seek to block the operations of a company that contributes to climate change, and even go so far as to shutter it. But we cannot seek in the name of retribution to prevent the company's employees from finding other work. (Once again, there are exceptions. Perhaps the company owners, if they knowingly sought to contribute to the destruction of the environment, should receive adequate punishment before being allowed to pursue other projects.)

We have focused here on the particular intrinsic value associated with human beings. This is because we are interested in the common space of politics, a common space that centrally concerns humans. Before turning to our second type of dignity, we should note in passing that the intrinsic value we have described here is not the only type of intrinsic value there is. In chapter 4 we considered another form of intrinsic value, although we didn't call it that. The capacity for suffering seems to confer an intrinsic value on many living beings, a value that humans also embody but that isn't limited to humans. We might say that that capacity is implicit in parts of the description of human dignity that we have considered here, while for nonhuman animals that capacity is more limited. Although nonhuman animals, like us, require food, sleep, and shelter, and many of them need significant relationships with others, rarely do they engage in the kind of long-term projects characteristic of human life. To treat most nonhuman animals with dignity, then, is to acknowledge and respect their capacity for suffering.

So far we have discussed the side of dignity concerned with those whom nonviolence seeks to confront. The other side concerns ourselves as political actors. It is a matter of dignified behavior. How can we act in a dignified way in the space we share with others? One way to think of this is that we seek to create ourselves as models of political behavior, that we behave in such a way that we would be happy for others to emulate. To act with dignity is to navigate through common space in a way that others, unless they were too blinkered by their own views, would not find repulsive or embarrassing or that one would not be embarrassed to see in another. Lashing out verbally or physically against others, placing them in humiliating circumstances, spreading lies or rumors about them, trying to blackmail or extort from them, intimidating thcm for no important political end: all these are examples of undignified behavior that a person seeking to act nonviolently would reject. If dignity involves the recognition of the intrinsic value of another, it also involves a certain way of moving through shared space that can act as a standard for others to emulate and that one can look back on without regret.

If dignity is one of the values associated with nonviolence, equality is the other. The idea of equality is one that has run like a thread through the previous chapters and has a hallowed place in US history, stretching back to the Declaration of Independence's second paragraph, "We hold these truths to be self-evident, that all men are created equal." (Although we should note the term *men* and its implicit reference only to certain men.) It is the presupposition that each of us is equally capable of creating a life for ourselves and that this capacity should figure foremost in our political considerations. Or, to put it in terms we have just seen, it would be the idea that nobody has greater intrinsic worth than anyone else.

We should be clear about what this means, since it is easy to misunderstand. As we have seen, to say that people are equal is not to say that everyone deserves the same thing. Recall our example of the two people and the aspirin. Nor does it mean that what people do in their lives doesn't have any bearing on what they deserve, that everyone deserves equal respect regardless of how they act. Equality in the sense we are speaking of here is neither about need nor deservingness. It is instead about recognizing that all individuals have an intrinsic value, a value that they bear simply by being alive as human beings (or, in a different way and with a different value, nonhuman animals). This value does not render their actions irrelevant as to how we should treat them. A person can be punished for committing crimes, and at the limit may be liable to be killed in self-defense. (Does recognizing the value of equality prohibit capital punishment? That would be a larger debate, but I suspect the answer is yes.) But it does require that, however I act, I recognize the other as just as much a person as I am and act out of that recognition.

This presupposition of the equality of everyone can, as we have seen, lead us toward a position of extreme altruism. If everyone has equal intrinsic value, shouldn't I treat everyone as equal to me and therefore not allow myself or those I care about any greater moral regard than a stranger (assuming that the stranger hasn't done anything wrong)? That is precisely the position of the altruist, and what we are seeking here is decency rather than altruism. Would nonviolence then require of us an altruism that would be impractical for most of us to achieve?

In the case of nonviolent political action, I don't believe that altruism is necessary, nor that the presupposition of equality requires it. The presupposition of equality arises in a particular political context, one in which the adversary (whether individual or institutional) is committing oppressive actions against others. This adversary has already engaged in unjust behavior. The question we are considering is one of how to treat the other in our opposition to them, given that what they have done is morally compromised. We are not, as it were, starting from a zero point at which everyone is morally okay and therefore deserves equal moral consideration, which would be the assumption of extreme altruism. So in recognizing the equality of everyone, we do not have to place everyone on the same moral ground. Rather, what we need to do is to recognize the equal *intrinsic value* of everyone, their equal dignity as human beings, and use that to inform our actions. To put it another way, one that the philosopher Kant would fine congenial, we cannot treat others simply as means to our ends but must recognize them as ends in themselves.

As we can see, the values of dignity and equality, although distinct, are bound together. Everyone has dignity, that is the capacity to engage in projects and relationships, and so on. Moreover, everyone has it equally, or at least that is the presupposition under which we must operate. Any nonviolent political intervention must respect these two values. As a philosophical position then, we have a grasp of the framework of nonviolence. It offers us a way to conceive action that confronts the onerous actions of others while retaining the stance offered by civility.

NONVIOLENCE IN PRACTICE

Of course there are myriad ways in which a nonviolent politics could unfold, well beyond what could be addressed in a single volume.[12] However, we can get a sense of what this might look like if we consider two different arenas, that of an individual acting oppressively and that of an oppressive institution or structure. Thinking about these two arenas will give us a sense of how we might act in a politically decent way in uncomfortable political situations, situations in which we probably ought to do something to shape our common space but which will likely meet resistance from others.

In one sense, confronting individual prejudice or discrimination is often more emotionally fraught than confronting institutional or structural oppression. Attending a demonstration or writing a letter or email to a congressperson or boycotting a company is anonymous; you don't have to look into anybody's face and tell them they're doing wrong. Of course this is not always the case. Meeting with a congressperson or finding oneself across the table from an officer of a company engaged in polluting is a face-to-face encounter. Alternatively, one can, as we will see in a moment, confront an individual by going around them. However, there remains the individual—this person—whom one is confronting, either directly or indirectly.

To home in on the idea, we need to give a little detail to the possibility of individual nonviolent confrontation. After all, nobody confronts a person outside a specific set of circumstances. The individual one confronts has done or said something specific. They have uttered a racist remark to a group of like-minded individuals, or alternatively said something racist to a person of another race. (To keep things simple, we'll stick with racism, recognizing that homophobia, sexism, religious intolerance, blaming the poor, and so on, could all be substituted here—and also recognizing that the very concept of race is a contested one, and rightly so.) Or they have ignored a person of another race who sought their help, or actively impeded them in some way. Or they have encouraged others to discriminate against people of another race or been physically aggressive or not carried out their job responsibilities or voted for someone who is racist.

Moreover, the actions people commit occur in a larger context. The person who acts in a racist manner may be the supervisor of the person who is their object, a public official, a colleague, a stranger, or occupy another social role. And they will have a relation to me as a potential confronter as well. They may be *my* supervisor or colleague, a public official with whom I must interact or a perfect stranger. Finally, there is the crucial issue of whether I am a member of the class of people who are the object of the behavior. All these particularities play a role in structuring a decent response to racist behavior. Since we can't canvass all of them, let's look at three of the more common ones: a colleague expresses a racist sentiment in the absence of the object of their remark, a public official is treating a person of another race poorly, or a stranger is verbally aggressive toward someone of another race. The sketches of these scenarios will necessarily be brief, but I hope they bring out salient aspects of a nonviolent response.

In all these sketches I will assume that the person who is called to confrontation is not a member of the class of people who are the object of the behavior. That is, in common parlance, I want to ask what it is to be a decent ally. The question of confronting someone who is attacking you as a member of a certain class is a distinct one, and, as a privileged white male, I wouldn't feel comfortable weighing in on that scenario without a whole lot of caveats. As it stands, there will be caveats enough as we proceed.

The first example is probably the most common. What

does one do when a colleague—either at work or in a social situation—expresses a racist sentiment? Recall here that we are not in a situation of persuasion. The person is committed to their racism, even if, as is usually the case, they deny that they're racist. "I'm not racist but is it really an accident that blacks always blame others for their own inability to get ahead?" "Have you noticed that Indians just happen to smell bad?" "Don't you find Safiya's head scarf a bit unnerving?" "Jian is an awful driver; what is it with the Chinese and driving?" We've all been around comments like this, often in situations in which the social ethos dictates just going along, not risking the awkwardness of a confrontation.

There are those who counsel always confronting the person at that time. If the person is indeed committed to their racism, that's probably what should occur. It's uncomfortable, to be sure, but a moment of social awkwardness would seem a small enough price to pay for blunting racist behavior, particularly in a situation, like ours in the US, in which racism is now able to be more openly expressed. Confronting a racist remark not only displays your own opposition to racism but also gives permission to others who are within earshot to oppose openly expressed racist sentiments. Moreover, it need not be done in a way that demeans the person themselves. "I find that comment to be offensive" probably works better than, "Wow, you're a full-on racist, aren't you?" At least most of the time.

Of course, such confrontation is often met with a denial of some sort: "I was just kidding. Can't you take a joke?" But once the social awkwardness has been introduced, it's easier to remain in it. Replying that one doesn't find such jokes to be very funny is not likely to add to the discomfort that has already been introduced into the situation. Moreover, it usually feels better to stand one's ground once that ground has been established than to back off.

The situation we're imagining here is one where the person uttering the remark is a racist. Often, however, things are more complicated than that. People express racist attitudes unknowingly. After all, as we have seen, we are all products of a social, political, and cultural environment (in truth, a number of them). Many of us are creatures of good will who may embody attitudes that we would reject if we reflected on them. There are those who say that this fact is irrelevant and that we should always confront racism when it occurs, regardless of the character of the person expressing it. I'm not convinced of this. If someone I know expresses a racism they would reject if they were aware of what they were saying, I think it's often more effective to wait for an opportunity to call them aside and explain what I saw in their behavior. We can think of it this way: public confrontation almost always leads to defensiveness. With an overt racist, such defensiveness is fine. The goal there is not to change the person but rather to fence off their ability to display their racism. By contrast, with someone who is unknowingly expressing a racist sentiment, making them defensive is less likely to encourage change then a sympathetic explanation in a more private venue. Recognizing that people of good will can also express racist sentiments—and so treating them also as people of good will—can go a long way toward encouraging personal reflection on their part.

How about where a public official is treating someone poorly? In a sense, this is an easier situation for confrontation. The norms of public behavior are that one should treat all people with equal respect. Suppose you find yourself in the unfortunate situation of being at a Department of Motor

Vehicles office, say renewing your driver's license, and you see one of the attendants treating an African American man rudely, more rudely than they are treating white folks. Several options are open to you at that point, depending on the specifics of the situation. You might go and stand next to the man and say that you think the employee is acting in a racist manner or is being deliberately rude. Or, slightly less confrontationally, you might ask the man himself if he is okay with how he's being treated. Or you might approach a supervisor and tell them what you're seeing. In all these scenarios it is probably best to let the person know you're standing with him. Being the object of prejudice, among other difficulties it creates, is humiliating. It makes a person feel alone. Acting in solidarity with someone who is undergoing prejudice reduces that sense of being naked before the world and with it the humiliation that accompanies being the object of egregious behavior.

All of this brings us back to themes we discussed in the second and third chapters. In a society like ours where racism is woven into our everyday social relationships, common decency involves a recognition that those of other races (genders, sexual orientations, and so on) are fellow citizens and should be treated as such. A mentor of mine once said that in a country like ours we are all at best recovering racists. He didn't mean just white folks, but everyone, because we're all brought up to think in not just racial but racist terms. It is worth carrying that wisdom with us as we navigate our routine interaction with others, seeking daily to recover from the racism that is part of the ethos of our common space.

It is also worth recognizing the role that race and other forms of oppression play in creating the need for certain forms of benevolence, and in being sensitive to the deleterious effects of certain forms of benevolence. In the third chapter we saw the conflict between benevolence and politics, between seeking to ameliorate difficult conditions and change or challenge the basis of those conditions. (Below we will see another aspect of their complicated relationship.) Both benevolence and political action run another risk, one that can reinforce racism. In a word, both can be patronizing, seeking to assist others on their behalf rather than alongside them. This, you will immediately recognize, is the phenomenon of the "white savior," the white person who "heroically" steps in and solves the difficulties facing African Americans because, one way or another, those African Americans could not do it themselves. This is what makes, for instance, the DMV example I just described a vexed one, one that requires reflection on the line between solidarity and patronizing behavior, a line that can be difficult to discern in concrete situations. In working on issues of race, I have made many mistakes that come from my own ignorance about this line. The best I can say for myself is that I hope I'm learning.

The phenomenon of the white savior is itself, of course, racist. This does not mean that white folks should not exhibit either benevolence or political solidarity with African Americans or other marginalized groups. Rather, that solidarity needs to be navigated carefully to avoid—to the extent possible—the racism that pervades the atmosphere in which our actions take place. There are, of course, vigorous debates about how best to do this, which I will leave to the side. I want only to note that in a society as racist as ours (and the US is hardly alone here), our attempts to act decently require us to remain aware of the character of our common space and how it might affect our own attitudes and actions.

The final scenario involves the confrontation of someone

who is verbally aggressive toward a person of another race. As I write this I am aware of a recent event that shows how dangerous this situation can be. A man was being verbally abusive to a woman with a headscarf, and when three other men sought to confront him about this he pulled out a knife, killing two of them and wounding the third.[13] One does not know what a stranger will do, particularly in at atmosphere as politically polarized and combative as in the US currently. Decency does not require us to risk our lives to prevent an act of racism. But it does ask us to do something. Too often people become frozen in these situations, watching them unfold but finding themselves unable to act. However, action is not always that difficult. If direct intervention is perceived as too threatening, one can often call an authority, someone with the ability to confront the aggressor more effectively.

Of course, there are situations in which it is less perilous to step in directly. The standard procedural advice in situations like this is to approach the object of the aggression directly and open a conversation about some neutral topic, avoiding eye contact with the aggressor. Confronting deep anger directly, particularly when one is alone, unless one is physically capable of defending oneself, can be a recipe for injury. However, removing the object of abuse is less often so. Going up to someone who is on the receiving end of some verbal abuse, sitting next to them, and asking whether they've seen the latest Hollywood blockbuster movie, can be a way to exhibit solidarity with them, confuse the aggressor, and consequently defuse the situation. It is, as all these situations are, a matter of judgment.

So far we have been discussing nonviolence in individual settings. Most nonviolence, though, takes place collectively and in opposition to institutional or structural oppression.

If we define it widely, it can range from a letter-writing campaign to a public official to voter registration to demonstrations to nonviolent civil disobedience, and everything in between. What all these share is that they involve action to change the character of our common space. That we share a common space characterized by various oppressions is hard to deny (although there will always be a few ready to deny it). The question then is how to act decently regarding those oppressions.

Before addressing that issue directly, it would be worth pausing over the importance of political action of this type. There is a tendency to think that politics is something that takes place *over there*. "Oh, I'm not into politics," many of us are tempted to say when asked to act in a way to intervene on our common space. But politics is never over there. It is always right here. We are all the products of our common space, with all its good and bad features. None of us, as we have seen, are immune to the cultural influences, social attitudes, or power relationships that structure that space. This does not mean that we are simply helpless before it, that we are mere products without any agency of our own. But it does mean that we cannot remove ourselves from the context in which our social relationships unfold. If, as we learned in the second chapter's discussion of the ethics of care, we are all formed in relationship to others, then we are all subject to social influences that may not determine us but whose influence we must recognize. We are all, at best, recovering racists.

Although someone might say, then, that they are not into politics, politics is nevertheless into them. It helps form them in ways that, upon reflection, they may or may not approve of. And that formation, in turn, makes them cocreators of the common space they occupy. Otherwise put, whether they like it or not, for the same reasons that politics are into them, they are into politics. We are all formed in relation to a common space that we in turn contribute to. The question, then, for each of us—both individually and collectively—is not whether but instead how to be into politics.

We might say that our relation to politics is one of both dissatisfaction and hope. We are dissatisfied with some aspect of our common space, whether it is racism or homophobia or economic inequality or something else. If we are of a different political orientation we might be dissatisfied with other aspects of our common space, say, a lack of greater economic liberty or too much social liberty. Political struggle occurs when opposing dissatisfactions meet or when a dissatisfaction with an aspect of common space meets a satisfaction with it. Nevertheless, none of us are ever entirely satisfied with the structure and ethos of our common space, which is to say that none of us feel—or are likely ever to feel—that we live in a utopia.

Political action, though, requires more than dissatisfaction. It also requires hope. If we are dissatisfied with an aspect of our common space and yet feel there is nothing to be done about it, we are unlikely to act. We may complain or feel trapped or cynical, but we will not be moved to action if we are convinced there is nothing to be done. If we are asking ourselves how to relate to our common space and to one another within that common space, we must feel that there are ways of relating that are possible for us. This is where hope comes in.

Politics, then, begins in dissatisfaction and hope and extends outward toward our shared space through the way we involve ourselves in it.

How might we act in a politically decent way regarding institutional or structural problems? There is, of course, no one answer to this. Moreover, any particular recommendation that I would have necessarily comes from my own political leanings, which are surely abundantly obvious by now. However, there are several things that we might say of a decent political involvement, for whatever issue or issues it is undertaken. First, there should be involvement—active involvement. If what I have said about politics is correct, we are all political beings, whether we care to be or not. Our various engagements and action are politically influenced and have political influence, even if to a minor degree. Decency would counsel recognizing that and asking ourselves how we might orient our engagements and actions to improve our common space.

This does not require a radical rethinking of who we are or what we are about. That would not be decency but instead extreme altruism. Rather, it asks of us that we try to leave our common space better off for our having participated in it throughout our lives. This can happen in many ways. For instance, one person I know in Greenville has organized demonstrations every Tuesday for over a year near the office of Senator Lindsay Graham. She invites others to contribute to the various themes of the Tuesday demonstrations. Sometimes they concern health care, at other times immigration rights, and at still other times wealth inequality. She publicizes the demonstrations, does outreach to remind people that they're happening, and makes people feel welcome when they show up. Hers is a creative response—one among many possible creative responses—to our current political situation.

If there is to be involvement, it should take on the lessons of the values of dignity and equality. This is the second point. Treating others as having lives to live, however much one disagrees with them (and with exceptions at the extreme, like self-defense or defense of others), acting in a dignified manner (which, recall, means acting like a model for political action, not walking around stiffly attired and with eyes pointed straight ahead), and recognizing the equal worth of everyone can frame political action, particularly in a time of polarization and political indecency. Dignity and equality do not tell us what to do, but they can guide us in our attempt to do it.

Finally, as with the benevolence we discussed in the third chapter, urgency matters. Just as there are environmental urgencies, there are political urgencies. (As many will immediately notice, environmental urgencies are also political urgencies.) Where racism is on the rise, as it seems to be in the US as I write these lines, confronting racism becomes more urgent. Political action, to the extent that it can, ought to privilege more urgent issues over less urgent ones. This is not to say that there shouldn't be other determinants as well. I am more likely to act effectively if I work on an issue that emotionally grips me than on one that does not. Urgency should be an important consideration in forming my political decisions, but it need not be the only one.

Having invoked the concept of benevolence, however, we might ask the question raised at the end of the third chapter regarding the balance between benevolence and political involvement. We saw there, and again briefly in this chapter, the conflict between those who seek to ameliorate current conditions and those who seek to change the structure of those conditions. This division, of course, is a little too neat. Certain kinds of benevolence might change the structure of a set of political conditions. Providing schooling for young women in countries with an egregious history of sexism would in effect challenge that sexism. Alternatively, changing the structure of a set of political conditions can ameliorate the effects of those conditions. In fact, that is often the goal of political change.

The deeper point to recognize here is there is no question of benevolence versus political action, since benevolence is a form of political action. Benevolence intervenes in our common space (or in the common space of another group of people), and in doing so has effects. These effects might not always be positive, as when benevolence comes in the form of patronizing help. (But then is it really benevolent?) However we act, whether through seeking to be benevolent or through political involvement for change, we are always affecting the common space in which we conduct our lives.

The question for us, a question that is necessarily political but also can be one of benevolence, is not whether to ameliorate current conditions or change them, but rather how we might act decently to improve our common space. This question need not lead us to extreme altruism. We do not have to ask it as a question of what the entirety of our lives should look like. But to one degree or another, each of us should ask it of ourselves and answer it in our action to the degree that is reasonable for us. Decency can ask no more but should ask no less of us.

OUR STORIES AND OUR VALUES

It is sometimes said that we live stories. Each life, we are told, follows a story line, one that can be recounted by the person living it or by others. But what does this mean? Does it mean that each of us is consciously creating a narrative for our lives, a story according to which we then act in order to realize it? That seems unlikely. I don't live like that, and I don't know anyone who does. Alternatively, does it mean that each of our lives can be rendered in terms of a particular story? Is the idea that there is a story there that characterizes each of our lives, a story that we may not know but that can be discovered through self-reflection, investigation, or perhaps by others? However, there are many different but adequate stories that can be told about a particular life. These stories may focus on different aspects of a person's life, or emphasize different events or facts, or bring forward different themes, or rely more or less on a person's self-understanding. Human lives are too rich to be reducible to a particular narrative that must be said to be the only one adequate to capturing its essence or its trajectory.

There is a different and more plausible way of approaching the issue. We might think of our lives as, in the term introduced by the philosopher Adriana Cavarero, narratable.[1] Our lives can be rendered as stories, but that rendering can happen in different ways. On the one hand, there isn't a single story there waiting to be told or discovered. On the other hand, however, not just any story can be told about our lives. There are, we might say, facts that constrain the kinds of stories through which our lives can be rendered.[2]

In this last chapter, I want to address the issue of our relation to stories, but from a different angle. Regardless of whether and how we live stories, we all *tell* stories about ourselves. Rarely are those stories about our lives as a whole, but just as rarely do we go a whole day without telling *some* story about what we're up to, if not to others then at least to ourselves. But why turn to stories at this point?

In the previous chapters we sought to understand moral decency in what we might call a centrifugal way. We have moved outward from ourselves toward others, close to us or distant in space, time, species, or beliefs about our common space. We have been looking toward others and asking about our moral relationship to them. In this concluding chapter, I would like to start by switching our angle of vision. Rather than gazing outward, let's turn our gaze inward for a bit, looking at ourselves before returning to an outward gaze. Throughout this book we have oriented ourselves around the theme that others have lives to live and that moral decency involves respecting that in our interactions with them. Taking a look at ourselves as storytellers, and particularly as tellers of stories about ourselves, will allow us to see this orientation in a different light, starting not from those to whom we are morally related but from ourselves as beings of—sometimes uncomfortable—moral complexities.

So, to begin, here's a (fictional) story:

> I was at the store this morning to buy some groceries. The person ahead of me in line had forgotten his wallet and was asking the store clerk whether he could buy his items on credit. After all, he argued, he shops there all the time and they surely recognize him. This discussion went on for five or six minutes.

As it stands, it isn't much of a story. Really, it is just a recounting of events. But now let me add another line:

> So I offered to pay for the groceries for him.

Or a different one:

> So I told him that there were other people in line behind him and that we had lives we wanted to get on with.

Adding either of these lines changes the character of the story. Now, instead of a minimal story about someone else, it becomes a story about me. But there is more. Not only is the story about me; it is a story that reveals me in a certain way. In fact, it reveals me in different ways, depending on which response I give. If I say, "So I offered to pay for the groceries for him," I am revealed as someone generous, and if I tell this story to someone else, I am seeking to reveal myself to them as generous. However, if I add the other line, things are more complicated. If I tell *this* story to someone else, how am I seeking to reveal myself? As someone who cares about other people and is irritated by those who don't? As someone who is willing to stand up to a rude carelessness? As someone who values order and is willing to confront disorder? Or am I just blowing off steam right after a frustrating moment?

And independent of how I *seek* to reveal myself, in telling the story to others what am I *actually* revealing of myself? For it might be that although, for instance, I seek to reveal myself as someone who values caring for others (that is, those in line behind me), I am really revealing myself as someone who doesn't feel that those who can't get their act together deserve the patience of others. I will return to the question of interpretation in a bit, but I first want to linger over something that might get lost if we jump right into that question.

In this story, simple as it is, with the addition of either line—the line that makes the story about me—I am revealing an aspect of who I would like to be or at least who I would like to be seen to be. I am placing before others, or maybe before myself, an image of myself that I consider valuable. I need not be aware that I am doing this. In fact, as we will see, it is sometimes the case that my stories about myself reveal aspects of what I value that I would not acknowledge if they were presented to me. That is to say, we can distinguish between what I seek to be revealing when I tell a story about myself and what I am actually revealing. However, in the story above the addition of either line presents me as valuing a certain mode of engagement toward the world. I would like to put the point this way: many of my stories (although certainly not all of them) express values of mine.

What is it to express a value through the telling of a story about oneself? To understand this, let's first investigate the idea of a value and then the idea of expression. It will turn out that they are deeply enough related that to understand either fully requires reference to the other, but we can get an initial grasp of the phenomenon we're trying to understand if we separate them for the moment. The term *value* can be used in many ways. There are, of course, moral values of the kind we have been discussing. But there are also aesthetic values like beauty and prudential values like caution. A little farther afield there are economic values and political values. Although my use of the term may overlap with one or another of these, I am trying to capture something here that is independent of them. I might put the matter this way: the values our stories about ourselves seek to express are ways of being in or ways of engaging the world that we endorse, identify with, or seek to embody.

This way of putting things involves three possibilities—endorsement, identification, or seeking to embody. The first is a matter simply of approval. In telling some stories I approve of the way of being I express. (Again, let's bear in mind a point to which we will return, that I might not acknowledge this approval.) In identifying with a way of being or engaging the world, I see myself as actually embodying that way I approve of. Alternatively, and this is the third possibility, it may be that in telling a story about myself I don't identify with it but rather seek to embody it. What all three have in common, however, is that the way of being I am expressing through a story (or several ways of being if the story is complicated enough) is something that I find valuable. I may not find it valuable for others, and so it need not be a moral value. However, I do find it valuable for myself. In short, I value it. That is what I mean here by the term *value*.

If we turn to the idea of expression, we should first steer clear—as we have already seen—of thinking of it as consciously expressing. In telling a story about myself I may be consciously trying to get you to think of me in a way I value, but that is not necessarily the case and, in fact, is probably the exception rather than the rule. We tell stories about ourselves all the time without reflectively constructing them in such a way as to have a particular influence on our audience, even when that audience is ourselves. More often, we tell stories to amuse, to share our lives, to reflect on what has happened to us or what we have done, to form bonds with others, or just to pass the time. Most of our stories don't so much announce our values as reveal them. It is through our stories that our values can be grasped.

How does this revelation occur? After all, our stories don't come labeled with values. If they did, then the story that ended with my telling the person in line that there were other people in line behind him and that we had lives we wanted to get on with would not be ambiguous between several interpretations. Our stories, then, or at least many of them, reveal values that must be interpreted to be understood. And here is the first overlap of the issue of telling stories about ourselves with that of the question of whether our lives are themselves stories. If our lives can be rendered as stories—if they are, in Cavarero's term, *narratable*—then one can ask which narrative or narratives are the accurate ones, or at least the most accurate ones. Just so, if our lives reveal our values, and if those values are not announced in the stories, then how do we tell which values are being revealed?

The broad answer is similar in both cases: it is a matter of interpretation. But we should be clear here and not fall prey to the temptation to think that interpretation is simply a subjective matter. There are a variety of constraints on interpretation that make some interpretations better than others. Of course, there will be cases in which the interpretation is obvious. When I tell a colleague a story about my recent discussion with a famous philosopher and, in relating the story, use the philosopher's first name in an offhand way, it should be clear—even if it isn't clear to me—that I value being seen as respected by significant or influential philosophers. And it is a short step from there to the recognition that I value that respect as well. It is unlikely that I would like to be seen to be respected by famous philosophers if I didn't think that that respect itself mattered.

Of course, there are exceptional cases that would make interpretation more complicated. Let's take this one. Perhaps I am trying to impress someone I want to date and think that she would find me more interesting if I were associated with well-known figures in the field, even though I don't really care about that. Then my wanting to be seen as respected by influential figures comes apart from actually wanting to be so respected. What might we say then about the values the story is revealing? To approach this question, I should note first how unlikely such a scenario is. It is a bit hard to imagine my wanting to impress someone with a story expressing a value that I myself don't endorse, identify with, or seek to embody. Stories told to impress others with values that one rejects seem to me to be more nearly cynical. And that is perhaps where interpretation should go. One value that might be getting expressed through this rendering of the story is that I endorse the value of manipulating others to my own ends. Now that value is likely one that I would not want to acknowledge even if I am in fact expressing it through my story. That would be a matter of self-deception, a point to which we will return.

For the moment, let's recognize that we have arrived at an important constraint on interpretation: the audience, or perhaps better, my conversational partners, since they may be active participants in my storytelling. In order to grasp the value a story is expressing, it's important to know the conversational partners for the story. To put the point another way, what I am trying to do with a story will often help reveal which value or values I am expressing, and that trying will, importantly, depend on the audience for the story. This is true even if the conversational partner is myself. For instance, when I tell myself a story about how my insulting a colleague in a way that might have been called rude was actually a bold standing up for principle in the face of his attempt to manipulate us all, I am likely revealing values of integrity as well as social cooperation, values that I would certainly endorse or else I would likely not have told that story to myself.

So far I have argued that many of our stories express values that we hold—that is to say, ways of being or engagements with the world that we endorse, identify with, or seek to embody. However, one might object here that many others of our stories don't seem to do that. In fact, they do the opposite. Rather than expressing values, they express something else. Take, for instance, the storyteller whose most common theme is how the world is arrayed against them. We all know the person for whom nothing ever goes right because that's the way the world is. I'm not talking here about people who really are the object of the world's onslaughts: exploited, marginalized, and impoverished people who, at least in my country, are too often blamed for the social conditions that oppress them. Instead, I'm thinking of people for whom the weather is never right, appliances are never fixed on time, the mail is too slow, their work is unappreciated, and their children never call. Can we really say of these people that they are expressing values in the stories to which they subject themselves and the rest of us?

I believe the answer to this question is yes. In fact, I think it is clearly yes. These stories express an identification with victimhood. People who tell these stories consistently, while they are perhaps really irritated by the events they recount, are usually stubbornly attached to seeing themselves as helpless objects of the world's vicissitudes. They can do nothing to make their lives better, because whatever they do it will not work out. The world assures them of this. People like this are attached to their status as martyrs to the world's unkindness, an attachment that is expressed in the stories they tell.

This is not to say that stories never express disvalues. If someone who does not identify with the role of victim tells a story in which they are the object of injustice, this would certainly express a value with which they resist identifying. Say, for instance, that a normally confident and open person tells you a story about being harassed by a police officer. This person doesn't identify with their victimization by the police, as may be evident from their history and probably from their affect when they tell the story. They are here expressing a disvalue, a normative position—that of victim—which they do not endorse, identify, or seek to embody. I take it, however, that such an expression of disvalue remains within the parameters of the position I'm articulating here. Through the expression of disvalue, a value is being negatively expressed or at least indicated. What the value is—or what those values are—may be difficult to tell, since it is not the identification but rather the disidentification that is being directly expressed. However, we remain on the same normative register. These stories, when not expressing values we would endorse, are expressing values we reject in favor of others.

Before going any further, let me be clear about one thing. I'm not claiming that the only thing our stories about ourselves do is express values. And I'm not claiming that *all* our stories about ourselves express values. Rather, I'm pointing to the idea that many of our stories express values, and that we can learn a lot about our values by investigating those stories.

Let's return for a moment to our victim. Although for all the world this victim may be expressing their identification with his victimhood through their stories, they may well refuse to acknowledge that as one of their values. "No," they tell us, "it's not me. The problem is the world. I really wish life were otherwise, that things worked out better. But the world is just badly arrayed, and so I find myself always on the short end." Such talk can be frustrating, since one wants to point out the disconnection between the stories this person tells and the refusal to acknowledge the value that is constantly expressed. However, it is precisely this disconnection I want now to focus on. One of the aspects of the stories we tell about ourselves—illustrated in the extreme by the victim in my example—is that they can reveal values that we would prefer not to acknowledge, even to ourselves. Otherwise put, our stories can express our self-deceptions.

I want to tread this territory of self-deception carefully, since it is easy to go wrong when discussing it. I believe that the approach to self-deception through this account of the stories one tells about oneself can loosen the grip of other, less satisfactory approaches. I'm thinking here especially of a psychoanalytic approach, one for whom stories are often traceable back to a particular trauma, that of the Oedipal stage. For the classic psychoanalyst at least, the self-deception revealed in our stories about ourselves is symptomatic of—or at least associated with—an early conflict that analysis can trace back to its origins. On the account I am defending here, there need be no deep reason, one situated in the dark recesses of childhood, for a particular self-deception. To see this, let me offer a quick, embarrassing story, one that I told my wife right after it happened.

I was driving home one day after working out at my local gym when a car pulled out in front of me. It came close to cutting me off as it turned onto the road and then proceeded to go ten miles an hour under the speed limit. So I laid on my horn for a good quarter of a mile while I followed him. (Notice the "so." "So I laid on my horn." That's a New York "so." For New Yorkers it just follows that if someone makes a move like that you lay on your horn.)

In any event, if I reflect honestly on this story it reveals a value that I would be loath to claim publicly, which is why it is embarrassing. It is a lapse into a certain aggressiveness of the kind that I mentioned above. However, I think a lot of males, particularly in the US, share this aggressiveness as a value, even if it is one they would not want to acknowledge. If my wife had pointed out at the time that I seemed to value my aggressiveness toward this person—which, mercifully, she did not—I would have certainly denied it. I might have said something about what a jerk the driver was, or what we New Yorkers are like, but would not have admitted that I sometimes express a value that I find repulsive in much of our culture. But the fact is, I do express that value sometimes. It is part of who I am, even though I would rather it not be and would probably continue to deny it in many of its other expressions.

The philosopher Richard Moran tells us, "The truth of someone's story will typically display forms of significance that could not be available to the character, but without for all that being either a falsification or the representation of something that applies only to the story and not to the reality the story is recounting."[3] However, there is no need to find the seeds of this unavailability in childhood conflicts. It need not be, for instance, that my father was some sort of castrating type that I find myself expressing this value that I cannot acknowledge, even to myself. Rather than looking inward at deeply buried conflicts in my childhood to see the source of this self-deception, we should instead look outward at our cultural norms.

In his book *Freudian Repression*,[4] Michael Billig, for all his praise of Freud, finds the seeds of repression to lie not in the individual's unconscious but, rightly in my view, in those social and cultural norms that dictate what one can say and what one cannot. Although a full treatment of this point and its implications for thinking about self-deception is beyond what I can discuss here, let me just call attention to the idea that in any culture there are things that are allowed to be admitted to others and things that are not. And because of this, there will be things that can be admitted to oneself and things that cannot. Otherwise put, the roots of repression, and with it self-deception, are social rather than individual.

This can be seen clearly in the story I have just told you. In much of US culture at large, such aggressiveness is often welcomed. If I were immersed in that culture I would have been able not only to admit to myself that I laid on the horn for so long; I might have been able to boast of it. But that isn't the culture in which I find myself, for which by the way I am eternally grateful. Rather, my culture, or perhaps subculture, is one in which such aggressiveness—indeed rudeness—is frowned upon. It is not okay among the people I prefer to spend time with to act in this way. And so it is difficult to admit, even to myself, that I can hold acting this way as a value. However, my telling the story I told shows that while I reject that value consciously, there is part of me that still holds it as a value. And, in a wider culture that encourages men to be macho and aggressive, this should not be entirely surprising. After all, my subculture may reject the values of the larger culture, but we who inhabit my subculture are not immune to the influence of larger cultural norms.

There is, I believe, a lesson to be drawn from this consideration of how our stories can reveal aspects of ourselves that we would prefer not to acknowledge even to ourselves. It is the first of two lessons I want to consider, and the one that flows most obviously from what has just been said. We are more complicated, often in ways we would prefer not to acknowledge, than we would often like to believe. Investigating the stories we tell about ourselves is one way to reveal this to us. In fact, it is a privileged way of revealing this, since it is we who tell the stories. These are not stories that are told to us by others, but rather our own stories out of our own mouths. I need to be clear here, since putting things this way may invite a misunderstanding. As Adriana Cavarero has shown, many of our stories don't originate with us. They are told to us by others. In her book *Relating Narratives*, where she also introduces the idea of narratability, she argues convincingly for this. In her view, we seek to have meaningful stories of our lives told to us by others and can feel a sense of completion or wholeness when they do. Moreover, many of the stories we tell about ourselves are rooted in stories about us that others have told us.

I believe Cavarero is right about this. The social character of our existence makes it inevitable. I am not the origin of all my stories. Rather, they are a product of the relationships I share with others. Nevertheless, I do tell stories about myself, and those stories reveal values that I endorse, or identify with, or seek to embody. And, regardless of what I may wish, some of those stories reveal values that I would prefer not to acknowledge. That they come out of my mouth, however, gives them a particular privilege in revealing who I am that being told stories about myself by others does not possess. This does not mean that the stories others tell me about myself are necessarily less true than my own. Self-deceptive stories can reveal values that I hold while nevertheless being false or misleading. But, we might say, I *reveal* my values through my stories about myself whereas others *infer* my values through their stories about me.

The second lesson to be drawn from these reflections is complementary to the first, and important for an entirely different set of reasons. It is the lesson that will bring us back to moral decency and a recognition of others as having their own, more intricate, lives. If I am more complicated than I would like to believe, then others are also more complicated than they would like to believe. But, and this is the point, they are likely also more complicated than *I* would like to believe. The significance of this point should not be lost in a Europe and a United States that have become more polarized politically in ways we saw in the previous chapter.

We have a tendency to live in echo chambers that reflect our own righteousness back to us. Consider how embedded each of us is in our niche markets, our favorite internet sites and television channels, our isolated and sometimes gated communities, our social groups comprised of like-minded friends and colleagues. If the recent profusion of technological media has brought us all closer together in some ways, it has made it easier for us to distance ourselves from one another in others. We inhabit communities that reinforce our beliefs about ourselves and about those outside those communities, often with a sense of our own probity that we do not confer on the unfortunates who are not among us. If we take seriously the realization that we and others are more complicated than many of us think, a realization that reflecting on our stories about ourselves might lead us to, then we can counter this reductive thinking about others as well as about ourselves.

Once again, I need to be clear here. I am not endorsing any form of moral relativism that would see all forms of living or all types of belief as equally worthy. The previous chapters should suffice to quell any fear of that. And in fact, the phenomenon we are looking at here points in precisely the opposite direction. On the one hand, if we are more complicated than we might like to think, it is precisely because we may value things that we know we should reject and that reflectively we do reject. On the other hand, the complications of others may reveal to us aspects of them that we, *by our own normative lights*, would endorse. If others are more complicated than the echo chambers we live in would lead us to believe, this may well be because they endorse, identify with, or seek to embody at least some values that we ourselves also endorse, identify with, or seek to embody. And perhaps, by interacting with these others, we might find common ground that, if we listen only to ourselves, will remain unavailable to us. That is the point of civility we discussed in the previous chapter, and we arrive back at it through a reflection on ourselves, or more precisely on the stories we tell about ourselves.

We are all complicated creatures, living more than we know and at times more than we would like—or would like to know. We are, and so are others. None of us are seamless. None of us are without aspects of ourselves that we would often prefer to not to acknowledge, even to ourselves. If it is difficult for us to live up to the kinds of moral demands placed upon us by the extreme altruists of practice or moral theory, it is even difficult—perhaps impossible—for us to live up entirely to the sense we have of who we are. This need not be a deep source of worry to us. If we are willing to admit this to ourselves, then we do the best we can to figure out who we are and go on from there.

When we recognize this in others, however, we might become attuned to more than their fallibility. That itself would be something, if we see it not as a fault but as something that makes them more like us. Beyond their fallibility, though, we might recognize their complexity, a complexity that may make them more like us than we often imagine. It is one thing to tell oneself in the abstract that another person is, as a human being, like us in important ways. It is another and deeper thing to *feel* it in others the way we can feel it in ourselves. Using the stories we tell ourselves as the beginning of a reflection on our complexity as well as our self-deceptions can bring us to a point where the feel of that recognition becomes salient for us, a point insisted on by the ethicists of care we saw in the second chapter.

So where, finally, does this leave us? If the reflections of these pages have resonance for us, we find ourselves in a space that is one neither of moral purity nor moral depravity. Rare among us is the creature who scales the moral heights. Such exemplars exist, but most of us are not among them. I know that I am not, and those few I know who think they are strike me as quite mistaken. But neither are most of us pure egoists, seeking to benefit ourselves, others be damned. We don't think of ourselves that way and we are right not to think of ourselves that way. Our moral lives lie somewhere in between these two extremes. Moreover, although we are not likely or even able to craft ourselves to be our morally best, most of us are open to become morally better.

What this book has sought to do is to occupy that space between moral purity and moral depravity and to ask how we ourselves might occupy that space, the space of moral decency. In doing so it has aimed both to describe our moral lives in ways that are consonant with how we think of them and at the same time to suggest routes that, without abandoning what is dear to us, would open us to possibilities of moral growth.

This is not, as we saw in the first chapter, a task that has been taken up by much of traditional moral philosophy. This does not mean that such philosophy is on the wrong track. It is important to ask questions not only about the better and the worse but also about the best. But for those of us who pursue something less than the best, because we cannot or will not or perhaps think we ought not to do otherwise, what we have described here offers one way to think about our moral lives. Decency, if nothing more, is also nothing less than a way to conduct our lives that, if not optimal, might at least offer us a sense that perhaps we will leave this polarized, conflicted, and often fraught world a little better off for having passed through it.

NINE RULES FOR MORAL DECENCY THAT SHOULD BE FOLLOWED STRICTLY AND WITHOUT EXCEPTION

1. Look people in the face more often, particularly when you're angry with them.
2. If your colleague leaves the room, cover their cup of coffee with a napkin.
3. Enjoy your moral behavior as best you can.
4. If you're not going to give money to that homeless person, send it to an organization for the homeless.
5. Try not to contribute to the dying of the environment.
6. Say hello to the cat. Avoid eating it if possible.
7. Continue on your path of being a recovering racist, misogynist, homophobe, and so on.
8. Create some politics. After all, it created you.
9. Enjoy reading philosophy, even when it advises you to be better than you can reasonably be.

ACKNOWLEDGMENTS

This book arose out of a suggestion from my editor at the University of Chicago Press, Elizabeth Branch Dyson. Her faith in my ability to write it, her guidance throughout, and her suggestions on the initial manuscript were all more generous than I deserve. My wife, Kathleen, read each chapter and made suggestions that far improved what I had handed her. My colleague Chris Grau offered a close read of the first chapter that significantly improved its presentation. Jenni Fry's copyediting significantly improved the readability of the text. And two readers for the Press made close and sensitive readings from which I took a number of suggestions.

The book is dedicated to Kathleen, David, Rachel, and Joel, each of whom has taught me far more about moral decency than I should have needed to learn.

NOTES

PREFACE

1 These examples come from Peter Singer's *The Most Good We Can Do: How Effective Altruism Is Changing Ideas about Living Ethically* (New Haven, CT: Yale University Press, 2015). We will meet Singer again periodically throughout this book.

CHAPTER ONE

1 In case this might seem like a cultural quirk rather than an acknowledgment of others, it should be borne in mind that it is an example of the Scandinavian view that one is obliged to the community, in contrast to a US view that is typically more concerned with the rights one can claim upon the community.

2 Recently there have arisen a number of ethical approaches that resist the overall theorization that follows here. Among these is ethical particularism, especially as it appears in Jonathan Dancy's fascinating *Ethics without Principles* (Oxford: Clarendon Press, 2006). Although my approach here shares with Dancy's a resistance to overarching principles, it treads on different ground. Dancy is interested in articulating a proper approach to ethics in general; this book is focused on living a morally decent life.

3 Immanuel Kant, *Groundwork of the Metaphysic of Morals*, trans. H. J. Paton (New York: Harper and Row, 1964), 88.

4 In *Groundwork*, Kant's specific example concerns not dishonesty generally but lying specifically. However, it would seem that willing dishonesty

can no more be universalized than willing lying. There might be cases in which someone might not tell the entire truth without violating the categorical imperative, say when you are asked by a friend whether he looks good in his wedding pictures and you respond, "Your suit is really nice." But even here you can't will dishonesty but rather must will a certain limited type of honesty.

5 What we have seen here falls under Kant's category of "perfect duties." There are also "imperfect duties," those we need to perform but not all the time.

6 Perhaps the most influential recent text in virtue ethics is Bernard Williams's *Ethics and the Limits of Philosophy* (Cambridge, MA: Harvard University Press, 1985).

7 Aristotle, *Nichomachean Ethics*, 2nd ed., trans. Terence Irwin (Indianapolis, IN: Hackett, 1999), 1098a15.

8 Bernard Williams emphasizes this point in his contribution to *Utilitarianism: For and Against* (J. J. C. Smart and Bernard Williams, Cambridge: Cambridge University Press, 1973).

9 Peter Singer, "Famine, Affluence, and Morality," *Philosophy and Public Affairs* 1, no. 3 (Spring 1972), 231. Singer's argument has been developed at greater length by Peter Unger in *Living High and Letting Die: Our Illusion of Innocence* (Oxford: Oxford University Press, 1999). Shelly Kagan's *The Limits of Morality* (Oxford: Oxford University Press, 1991) comes to similar conclusions but uses different argumentative approaches.

10 Singer, "Famine, Affluence, and Authority," 231.

11 Singer, "Famine, Affluence, and Authority," 241.

12 Singer does not believe that we should treat all *persons* with equal respect but rather all *interests* equally. If, for instance, a one person has greater interests at stake than another, those interests should be privileged. This is the source of both of Singer's most controversial claims: that animal suffering should be treated as just as deserving of moral consideration as an equal amount of human suffering, and that the cognitively disabled should (since they have fewer cognitive interests at stake) be treated more like nonhuman animals. We will return to these ideas in chapter 4.

13 This is a simplified version of an argument offered by Garrett Cullity in *The Moral Demands of Affluence* (Oxford: Oxford University Press, 2004).

14 This is a version of an argument offered by Susan Wolf in her article

"Moral Saints," reprinted in her book *The Variety of Values: Essays on Morality, Meaning, and Love* (Oxford: Oxford University Press, 2015).

15 See, for instance, Michael Slote's *Beyond Optimizing: A Study of Rational Choice* (Cambridge, MA: Harvard University Press, 1989). A different approach is offered by Samuel Scheffler in *The Rejection of Consequentialism* (New York: Oxford University Press, 1982). He argues that consequentialism should allow for certain "agent-centered prerogatives," something akin to small moral holidays.

16 Although I should note that Shelly Kagan, in his book *The Limits of Morality* (Oxford: Clarendon Press, 1989), has offered some interesting arguments in favor of the idea that we should harm one innocent person if it will save two others.

17 Many years ago, for instance, I constructed a form of consequentialism that would avoid this recommendation. See chapter 2 of *The Moral Theory of Poststructuralism* (University Park: Penn State Press, 1995).

18 This again refers to Kant's "perfect" rather than "imperfect" duties, the latter of which do admit of the more and the less.

19 I discuss these at length in chapters 3 and 4 of *A Significant Life*.

20 There is another problem with this approach. It is not clear that any such list of duties would give us proper moral guidance. In an article aptly entitled "Above and Below the Line of Duty," the philosopher Susan Wolf argues that there are times when acting contrary to duty would be better and perhaps even required, and times when it is permissible not to perform one's duties. In her argument, she appeals to examples that we have already seen, using them to show that duties, while good rules of thumb, do not always provide the right moral guidance.

Regarding the first, she asks us to consider a situation in which, on the way to our office hours, we see a frail old man inside a house that is on fire. We can save the old man and there is no one else to do it. "Now," she writes, "it is generally believed that one does not have a duty to rush into a burning building to save the life of a stranger. But surely it would be absurd to be deterred from this act by the thought that one *does* have a duty to keep office hours" ("Above and Below the Line of Duty," in *The Variety of Values*, 207). Here it would be better to act contrary to duty; however, if one is not willing to do so, surely it cannot be *for the reason* that one has a competing duty to be present at office hours. The duties here cannot determine how we should act.

Alternatively, she asks us to imagine you are in your office hours "when you get a call telling you that your philosophical heroine is in the States on a rare visit. In fact—the caller here apologizes for the late notice—she is giving a lecture this very afternoon at another university in a nearby town. There would even be a place for you at dinner" (210). Here it would seem permissible to act "below the line" of duty rather than, as in the previous case, above it.

All this, as Wolf mentions, is not to deny that there are duties or that we should for the most part fulfill them. Her point instead is that thinking in terms of duties cannot act as the final arbiter of what we should or should not do, or of what is and is not permissible. As she puts the point, "there is a line of duty, but it is, necessarily, a dotted line" (200). If we are to understand our moral space aright, we cannot simply rely on a set of duties to tell us its contours.

21 To pick one of many examples, Thomas Nagel gets at a similar idea in *The Possibility of Altruism* (Oxford: Clarendon) when he writes, "Recognition of the other person's reality, and the possibility of putting yourself in his place, is essential," 83.

22 Todd May, *Nonviolent Resistance: A Philosophical Introduction* (Cambridge: Polity Press, 2015), 51.

23 Singer, "Famine, Affluence, and Authority," 231.

24 Aristotle, *Nichomachean Ethics*, 1094b25.

25 Those who are familiar with the history of moral philosophy will see parallels between the structure of my discussion and those of the eighteenth-century philosopher David Hume; others will find resonance with the thought of the ancient Chinese philosopher Confucius. For Hume, morality is rooted in the sympathy people have for their immediate fellows. "Sympathy," he writes, "is the chief source of moral distinctions" (David Hume, *A Treatise of Human Nature*, ed. David Fate Norton and Mary J. Norton [Oxford: Oxford University Press, 2000], 394). Sympathy, however, is local. It arises with those in our immediate surroundings. There is no such thing as an abstract love of justice or sympathy with those who are distant from us. Therefore, "the sense of justice and injustice is not deriv'd from nature, but arises artificially, tho' necessarily from education and human convention." We start from sympathy toward those immediately around us, and through "education and human convention" can extend and modify that sympathy such that we can form a sense of justice regarding our larger social setting.

Confucius view was similar. For him, the proper form of moral development starts from the right relation to one's family and extends outward from there. (I am indebted to an anonymous reader for calling my attention to this point.)

Although my approach is like Hume's and Confucius's in that way, I don't want to claim that our moral relations to others necessarily unfold through the extension and modification of sympathy or empathy or proper filial relationships. As we will see in chapter 2, there are debates about the respective roles of empathy and reason in grounding our moral relations with others. The parallels with Hume and Confucius are methodological rather than substantial; that is, they are grounded in ease of presentation rather than in a particular commitment to how morality develops or emerges within us. It may be that a moral sense or moral commitments arise differently for different people. I simply don't know. The only commitment I have to this way of proceeding—from the morally near to the morally more distant—is that it will be easier to present things that way. My goal is not to offer a theory of moral development but only a framework for thinking about mundane moral activity.

CHAPTER TWO

1 The account here, including the quotes, is taken from Eli Saslow, "The White Flight of Derek Black," *Washington Post*, October 15, 2016, https://www.washingtonpost.com/national/the-white-flight-of-derek-black/2016/10/15/ed5f906a-8f3b-11e6-a6a3-d50061aa9fae_story.html.

2 See Black's discussion in the *New York Times*, "Why I Left White Nationalism," November 26, 2016, https://www.nytimes.com/2016/11/26/opinion/sunday/why-i-left-white-nationalism.html.

3 Among the most famous philosophers to write about the face of the other is the French thinker Emmanuel Levinas. See, for instance, *Totality and Infinity: An Essay on Exteriority*, trans. Alphonso Lingis (Pittsburgh, PA: Duquesne University Press, 1969). He thinks of the experience face of the other as involving a confrontation with the other's infinite otherness. In contrast, I think the experience is not something other, but rather something like Hume's sympathy, discussed in the previous chapter. Rather than alterity it is an intimate sense of similarity that we are faced with. I argue for this in chapter 3 *Reconsidering Difference: Nancy, Derrida, Levinas, Deleuze* (University Park: Penn State Press, 1997).

4 John Protevi, "The Act of Killing in Contemporary Warfare," in *Life*,

War, Earth: Deleuze and the Sciences (Minneapolis: University of Minnesota Press, 2013), 62, 65. Levinas offers a biblical interpretation of this idea when he writes, "The first word of the face is 'Thou shalt not kill.'" Levinas, *Emmanuel, Ethics and Infinity: Conversations with Philippe Nemo* (Pittsburgh, PA: Duquesne University Press, 1995), 89.

5 For more on Mitch Snyder's life, see https://en.wikipedia.org/wiki/Mitch _Snyder.

6 These examples have been gathered from other articles by Yotam Benziman in "The Ethics of Common Decency," *Journal of Value Inquiry* 48, no. 1 (2014), 87–94. His purpose in the piece is to offer a general interpretation of the role of common decency in reinforcing the fabric of society. A sensitive discussion of common decency is offered by Cheshire Calhoun in her essay, "Common Decency" in *Moral Aims: Essays on the Importance of Getting It Right* (Oxford: Oxford University Press, 2016). There she casts common decency as essential to a "minimally well-formed agent." Another interesting discussion is provided by John Kekes in chapter 3 of *Moral Tradition and Individuality* (Princeton, NJ: Princeton University Press, 1989). He distinguishes between "rule-following" decency and "identity-conferring" decency: "Rule-following decency is to do what social morality prescribes. Identity-conferring decency is to do so because the agent feels a deep allegiance to social morality" (84). The latter involves a more engaged relationship to one's fellows and the society in which one finds oneself.

7 *The Analects of Confucius*, trans. Arthur Waley (New York: Vintage Books, 1989), 86.

8 This is Benziman's point in the article.

9 Stanley Milgram, *Obedience to Authority* (New York: Harper and Row, 1974).

10 Aaron James, *Assholes: A Theory* (New York: Doubleday, 2014), 4–5.

11 James, *Assholes*, 23.

12 Modern social contract theory finds its roots in Thomas Hobbes' *Leviathan*, although it appears as early as Plato's *Republic*. Among more contemporary examples, T. M. Scanlon's *What We Owe to Each Other* (Cambridge, MA: Harvard University Press, 1998) is important, although the locus classicus for current discussion is John Rawls's *A Theory of Justice* (Cambridge, MA: Harvard University Press, 1971). One thing that has always annoyed me about the title of Scanlon's book, important though

the book is, is that it is grammatically incorrect. The proper title would be *What We Owe to One Another*, since it is a theory of social contract, not of duties owed between two people.

13 Singer, *The Most Good You Can Do: How Effective Altruism Is Changing Ideas about Living Ethically* (New Haven, CT: Yale University Press, 2015), 102.

14 Carol Gilligan, *In a Different Voice: Psychological Theory and Women's Development* (Cambridge, MA: Harvard University Press, 1982).

15 Here is a chart of his six stages.

PREMORAL LEVEL

Stage 1: Punishment-Avoidance and Obedience	Make moral decisions strictly on the basis of self-interests. Disobey rules if can do so without getting caught.
Stage 2: Exchange of Favors	Recognize that others have needs, but make satisfaction of own needs a higher priority

CONVENTIONAL LEVEL

Stage 3: Good Boy/Good Girl	Make decisions on the basis of what will please others. Concerned about maintaining interpersonal relations.
Stage 4: Law and Order	Look to society as a whole for guidelines about behavior. Think of rules as inflexible, unchangeable.

PRINCIPLED LEVEL

Stage 5: Social Contract	Recognize that rules are social agreements that can be changed when necessary.
Stage 6: Universal Ethical Principle	Adhere to a small number of abstract principles that transcend specific, concrete rules. Answer to an inner conscience.

SOURCE: https://thesacredprofession.wordpress.com/2012/08/31/classroom-management-kohlbergs-stages-of-moral-development/

16 Gilligan, *In a Different Voice*, 22.

17 Virginia Held, *The Ethics of Care: Personal, Political, and Global* (Oxford: Oxford University Press, 2006), 46.

18 Held, *Ethics of Care*, 10–12.

19 For more on Molly Rush's life, see Liane Norman's *Hammer of Justice: Molly Rush and the Plowshares Eight* (Eugene, OR: Wipf and Stock, 2016).

20 See "Does Empathy Guide or Hinder Moral Action?" in the Room for Debate section of the *New York Times*, http://www.nytimes.com/roomfor debate/2016/12/29/does-empathy-guide-or-hinder-moral-action.

21 Held, *Ethics of Care*, 41.

22 For an interesting and sensitive discussion of this issue, see Barbara Herman's "The Practice of Moral Judgment," in *The Practice of Moral Judgment* (Cambridge, MA: Harvard University Press, 1993).

23 Susan Wolf, "Morality and Partiality," in her book *The Variety of Values: Essays on Morality, Meaning, and Love* (Oxford: Oxford University Press, 2015), 41.

24 Wolf, "Morality and Partiality," 44.

CHAPTER THREE

1 Kant discusses benevolence in *The Groundwork of the Metaphysic of Morals* as an imperfect duty, that is, a duty that one performs when one can rather than all the time. So while for Kant telling the truth is a perfect duty—one can never lie—benevolence is an imperfect duty—one should engage in it when one can. The discussion of benevolence in this chapter has affinities with Kant's view, but it is grounded in a very different perspective on morality.

2 Kagan, *Limits of Morality*, 21, 22.

3 Kagan clarifies his conception of impartiality on pages 62–63, noting that by impartiality he means, "if one outcome is objectively better than another, it is so for everyone, and everyone has a reason to promote it" (62).

4 Wolf, "Morality and Impartiality," 42.

5 There is a complication here, which is why I added the word "largely." Wolf's conception of an impartial morality seems to be in conflict with the ethics of care discussed in the previous chapter. For Wolf, partial emotions such as love are outside an impartial morality, and sometimes in conflict with it. For Held, by contrast, caring is part of an adequate morality. She reserves the idea of justice for a more impartial view. The issue here is whether morality should or should not encompass partiality. On the one hand I believe there can be conflict between one's par-

tial feelings and morality. In the case of the mother hiding her child, Wolf writes, "To describe the woman's conflict as one *between* morality and the bonds of love seems to me to capture or preserve the split, almost schizophrenic reaction I think we ought to have to her dilemma" ("Morality and Partiality," 44). This seems right, at least to me. On the other hand, Held seems right in saying that care is an important component of our moral relationships toward others; care leads us toward acting more properly in regard to others (although recall the limits of empathy discussed in the previous chapter). My own way of resolving this tension is to say that care is an important component of our moral relations with others, particularly in face-to-face interaction, but that moral *judgment* should be impartial: that is, when asking about what should or should not happen or have happened in a situation from a *moral* perspective, one should occupy the impartial standpoint advocated by Wolf.

6 For more on this, see Barry Estabrook's *Tomatoland: How Modern Industrial Agriculture Destroyed Our Most Alluring Fruit* (Andrew Meel Publishing, 2011).

7 Stephen Gardiner, *A Perfect Moral Storm: The Ethical Tragedy of Climate Change* (Oxford: Oxford University Press, 2011).

8 This is from Parfit's *Reasons and Persons* (Oxford: Clarendon Press, 1984), 358.

9 He offers this solution in chapter 16 of *Reasons and Persons*, but in the following chapters considers a number of complications to his initial solution. Essentially, he argues that we need our moral considerations in these issues to be more "impersonal," that is, focusing on how much good we can contribute rather than the particular people who might or might not be affected. But as he admits, this solution works for future generations only where there would be the same number of people in one future scenario as in another. He wanted to work out how to think about "different number" scenarios but died before he could come up with a solution for that.

10 Chapter 5 of John Broome's *Climate Matters: Ethics in a Warming World* (New York: W.W. Norton, 2012) is what convinced me. Although Broome is clear that much of the onus for addressing climate change falls on governmental policy, his case for carbon offsets is a compelling one. After reading the book I emailed him to let him know that his was the

most expensive book I had ever read, costing me not only the list price
of $23.95 but an additional $1,000 a year.

CHAPTER FOUR

1 For a nuanced discussion of this conundrum, see Jeff McMahan's "Eating Animals the Nice Way," *Daedalus*, 2008, 1–11.
2 The term was first introduced by James Rachels in his book *Created from
Animals: The Moral Implications of Darwinism* (Oxford: Oxford University
Press, 1990). He writes, "If we think it is wrong to treat a human in a
certain way, because the human has certain characteristics, *and a particular nonhuman animal also has those characteristics*, then consistency
requires that we also object to treating the nonhuman animal in that
way" (175). Moral individualism has been richly debated in philosophy.
One of its key recent defenders is Jeff McMahan. See, for instance, *The
Ethics of Killing: Problems at the Margins of Life* (Oxford: Oxford University
Press, 2002), esp. 203–32, and "Our Fellow Creatures," *Journal of Ethics* 9,
no. 3/4 (2005), 353–80.
3 A similar disturbing possibility is discussed in McMahan's *Ethics of Killing*, 359–60.
4 See http://www.projetogap.org.br/en/.
5 The philosopher Larry Temkin has complicated examples like this with
what are called "spectrum problems" in his book *Rethinking the Good:
Moral Ideals and the Nature of Practical Reasoning* (Oxford: Oxford University Press, 2015). For a summary of these, see the section on "Intransitivity and the Nature of the Good," on his wiki page, https://en.wikipedia
.org/wiki/Larry_Temkin.
6 Cora Diamond offers sensitive approaches to this issue in several
articles: "Eating Meat and Eating People," in Cass Sunstein and Martha
Nussbaum, *Animals Rights: Current Debates and New Directions* (Oxford:
Oxford University Press, 2004); "Experimenting on Animals: A Problem
in Ethics," in Cora Diamond, *The Realistic Spirit: Wittgenstein, Philosophy and the Mind* (Cambridge: Bradford Books, 1991) 335–65; and "The
Importance of Being Human," in David Cockburn, ed., *Human Beings*
(Cambridge: Cambridge University Press, 1991), 35–62.
7 McMahan gives this response to Diamond's work in "Our Fellow Creatures," 374.
8 Cora Diamond, cited in note 6 as an opponent of moral individualism,

is an example of someone who is at the same time sensitive to the needs and interests of nonhuman animals. See, for instance, the closing lines of "Eating Meat and Eating People," where she writes, "What might be called the dark side of human solidarity has analogies with the dark side of sexual solidarity or the solidarity of a human group, and the pain of seeing this is, I think, strongly present I the writings I have been attacking" (106).

9 This case is presented by Clare Palmer in her book *Animal Ethics in Context* (New York: Columbia, 2010). For a related but different approach, see Elizabeth Anderson's "Animal Rights and the Values of Nonhuman Life," in Sunstein and Nussbaum, *Animal Rights*, 277–98.

10 "The Era of 'Biological Annihilation' Is Underway, Scientists Warn," Tatiana Schlossberg, *New York Times*, July 11, 2017, https://www.nytimes.com /2017/07/11/climate/mass-extinction-animal-species.html.

11 See https://en.wikipedia.org/wiki/Temple_Grandin.

CHAPTER FIVE

1 For more on this, see https://www.nytimes.com/2017/02/01/us/uc-berke ley-milo-yiannopoulos-protest.html.

2 For more on this, see https://www.nytimes.com/2017/03/03/us/middlebury -college-charles-murray-bell-curve-protest.html.

3 Todd May, *Nonviolent Resistance: A Philosophical Introduction* (Cambridge: Polity Press, 2015), 51.

4 Much has been written on civility in politics. Two important recent works are Danielle Allen's *Talking to Strangers: Anxieties of Citizenship since Brown v. Board of Education* (Chicago: University of Chicago Press, 1996) and Mark Kingwell's *A Civil Tongue: Justice, Dialogue, and the Politics of Pluralism* (University Park, PA: Penn State University Press, 2008). Allen introduces the idea of "political friendship" as a friendship that must take place between people of very different viewpoints and orientations, often through various and complementary sacrifices. Kingwell's more traditionally philosophical work seeks to understand civil dialogue among those with very different views as a way to move toward more just social arrangements.

5 Lest we get too comfortable about the US's overcoming of slavery, until recently slavery of undocumented workers was practiced by a number of the tomato plantations in southern Florida. To learn about this, and

also about the courageous efforts of the Coalition of Immokalee Workers that ended the practice, see Barry Estabrook's *Tomatoland: How Modern Industrial Agriculture Destroyed Our Most Alluring Fruit* (Andrews McKeel Publishing, 2011).

6 See, for instance, the statistics in this *New York Times* editorial: https://www.nytimes.com/2017/07/29/opinion/sunday/black-income-white-privilege.html. For a fuller picture, Elizabeth Anderson's *The Imperative of Integration* (Princeton, NJ: Princeton University Press, 2010).

7 Among the numerous articles and books addressing this issue, see for example two short pieces from the *New York Times* in 2013: Eduardo Porter's "America's Sinking Middle Class" (http://www.nytimes.com/2013/09/19/business/americas-sinking-middle-class.html) and Annie Lowery's "The Rich Get Richer through the Recovery" (https://economix.blogs.nytimes.com/2013/09/10/the-rich-get-richer-through-the-recovery/). A longer analysis is offered in Heidi Schierholz and Lawrence Mishal's "A Decade of Flat Wages: The Key Barrier to Shared Prosperity and a Rising Middle Class" from the Economic Policy Institute (http://www.epi.org/publication/a-decade-of-flat-wages-the-key-barrier-to-shared-prosperity-and-a-rising-middle-class/).

8 An excellent and comprehensive history of recent nonviolent movements is Peter Ackerman and Jack Duvall's *A Force More Powerful: A Century of Nonviolent Conflict* (New York: St. Martin's, 2000).

9 Gandhi's term *satyagraha* (roughly translated as "truth-force") as he said, "was coined in South Africa to distinguish the nonviolent resistance of the Indians of South Africa from contemporary 'passive resistance' of the suffragettes and others" (*Non-Violent Resistance* [New York: Schocken Books, 1951], 3).

10 For more on this see my book *Nonviolent Resistance*, especially chapters 4 and 5.

11 This is a point insisted on in Joan Bondurant's remarkable study of Gandhian nonviolence, *The Conquest of Violence: The Gandhian Philosophy of Conflict* (Princeton, NJ: Princeton University Press, 1958), esp. 9–11.

12 In his magisterial three-volume *The Politics of Nonviolent Action* (Boston: Porter Sargent, 1973 [first two volumes] and 1985 [third volume]), Gene Sharp discusses a number of different ways in which nonviolent action can take place. His second volume, *The Methods of Nonviolent*

Action, offers nearly two hundred different methods, often with numerous examples.

13 Among the many articles covering this incident is Matthew Haag and Jacey Fortin's *New York Times* piece, "Two Killed in Portland While Trying to Stop Anti-Muslim Rant, Police Say," https://www.nytimes.com/2017/05/27/us/portland-train-attack-muslim-rant.html.

CONCLUSION

1 Adriana Cavarero, *Relating Narratives: Storytelling and Selfhood*, trans. Paul Kottman (New York: Routledge, 2000).

2 For some folks, the idea that there are facts there is just as implausible as the idea that there are stories there waiting to be told. Isn't the idea of uninterpreted facts just as controversial as the idea that there are stories waiting to be discovered? I am sympathetic to this hesitation. But even if we want to reject the idea that there are just uninterpreted facts, we will all probably still agree that certain things happen in our lives, however we conceive them, that constrain the kinds of stories we can tell about them.

3 Richard Moran, *The Story of My Life: Narrative and Self-Understanding* (Milwaukee, WI: Marquette University Press, 2015) 42–43.

4 Michael Billig, *Freudian Repression* (Cambridge, MA: Cambridge University Press, 1999).

INDEX